For Irene and Gerry

Contents

Acknowledgments

I am indebted to many people for their help in my research for this book, and particularly to those in Athlone and elsewhere who knew John Broderick personally and willingly shared their memories with me. The original John Broderick Committee, chaired by George Eaton, brought the man and his work back into the public consciousness in 1999 and encouraged my initial interest. George Eaton supplied some invaluable material from his personal archives. Gearoid O'Brien, who will recognize much of his own work in the early pages of this biography, has been endlessly helpful, encouraging and inspiring throughout the last four years, and has devoted many hours to finding press references and to putting me in contact with people who had stories to tell. Gearoid has also been responsible for supplying the majority of the photographs in the book and conveying them to the publishers by arcane technological means.

Of those to whom I have spoken in Ireland, I particularly valued the help and the time of Mrs Pat Drummond (née Coughlan), Father Cathal Stanley,

Acknowledgments

Archdeacon Patrick Lawrence, Mr Bert Heaton, Mrs Betty Claffey (née Hogan) and Mrs Maureen Doherty (née Hunt). Patrick Hunt sent several long and fascinating letters from his home in Toronto.

In London, Andrew Hewson opened up the files of the John Johnson Agency, shared his personal recollections of Broderick and continued to encourage me with his interest throughout the project. I had the good fortune to meet three of Broderick's long-suffering editors: Agnes Rook, Ken Thomson and Ken Hollings, all of whom for all the suffering remember him as a friend; and to speak at length to Elena Salvoni, whose very best stories were all off the record.

Foreword

In May 1999 the Athlone Rotary Club staged a celebration to mark the tenth anniversary of John Broderick's death. It was a convivial affair, spread over a weekend and involving a requiem mass, the naming of a street in Broderick's memory, and a great deal to eat and drink. Pride of place in the assemblage of notables bidden to attend was occupied by 'The Minister', Mrs O'Rourke TD, and 'Bishop John' of the diocese of Clonfert, to whom, I noted with interest, elderly men still raised their hats when they passed on the pavement.

The highlight of this commemoration was dinner at a restaurant overlooking the lake. Speeches were called for, and given. When they were over a gentleman rose unheralded from one of the side-tables and declared that he, too, wished to say a few words. The few words went on for some time, rather to the annoyance of the senior Rotarian at my side, but then there was a revelation. 'Not many of you will know', the speaker announced, with the air of one who imparts an absolutely sensational fact, 'that many years ago it was I who taught Bishop John to serve.' At this there was a kind of miniature explosion from the back of the room and a male voice shouted, 'Well, he went a bloody sight further in the Church than you did!' It struck me that what I had witnessed, here in Athlone, with the midlands twilight slowly descending around us, was a scene from one of Broderick's novels.

It would be presumptuous of me to claim that I knew John Broderick. I met him only once, at the very end of his life, and most of the assumptions I made about him on the strength of having read his novels I now find to be quite mistaken. If nothing else, Madeline Kingston's excellent study is a corrective to the idea that you can ever wholly understand a writer through his or her books. Back in 1987, scrabbling for a toe-hold on the rock-face of London literary journalism, I was reviewing novels for the newly established *Independent*. These were more spacious days for newspaper arts journalism, and the deputy literary editor, Robert Winder, had time to root around the new books and consider which of them might suit the tastes of his swarm of critics. And so there arrived on my desk, sometime in the early autumn, in its ghastly sapphire and grey jacket, a copy of Broderick's *The Flood*.

I had read nothing of Broderick's work before – not quite the shocking dereliction it sounds, as his English reputation never approached that of contemporaries such as Edna O'Brien and John McGahern – but *The Flood* seemed to me unlike any modern Irish novel I had ever come across: an individual blend of grim comedy, all done in glorious Athlone dialect, and secret grief built on a precise understanding of how the small-town midlands society of Broderick's childhood worked.

Not long after the review appeared, there came an appreciative letter from an address in Bath. This was followed by a correspondence and finally an invitation to lunch in London, which took place on a stifling day in early summer at Simpson's in the Strand. Damson-faced, solicitous beneath the winnowing fans, shuffling a little on a stick, Broderick looked like a man who was about to keel over with a stroke, which is exactly what he did a month or so later back in Bath. Phone calls made in the wake of this news were fielded by his legendary housekeeper Miss Scanlon. I never saw him again, and within a year he was dead. By chance a post-card from that era resurfaced the other day, in which Broderick showed an interest in William Trevor's novel, *The Silence in the Garden*. Sixteen years later it seems a signal from another world: a landscape full of excitement over new books and their writers, and famous Irish novelists taking one to lunch at Simpson's.

As *Something in the Head* makes plain in spades, Broderick was an intensely solitary man: the gaze that he turned on the Ireland of his day almost entirely backward-looking, the opinions that he pronounced, whether on Church or State, deeply conservative. 'How nice that John's written a good Catholic book,' the sisters of the Athlone convent were supposed to have remarked on hearing that Broderick's first novel was called *The Pilgrimage*. Despite a prohibition notice from the Censorship Board, it turned out that this was the literal truth. The roles into which he was cast by his upbringing were, you feel, deeply uncongenial to him (the local businessmen who watched his attempts to behave in a manner befitting the notional proprietor of the town's largest bakery laughed at what they called 'all that eejiting about') and fuelled the alcoholism that dominated his middle years. Going in search of him, in fact, one finds only a smokescreen of evasions and refusals to be drawn. Of his supposed homosexuality, or emotional career generally – and he was once quoted to the effect that 'I did everything I wanted in every conceivable way' – his biographer can only note 'no evidence of any sustained relationship at any time of his life'. Most of his deepest feelings, as Madeline Kingston discreetly shows, were put into his work, and it is the sense of this warm, sharp and somehow self-enclosed sensibility – an intelligence staring out from behind a high wall, reluctant in the last resort to join the world that teems beyond it – that gives a novel such as *The Waking of Willie Ryan* its distinction.

At the same time, it takes a visit to Athlone to establish what lies at the heart of Broderick's work. Mid-twentieth-century Irish provincial life has no better elegist. The grim Angevin Castle, the great midland plain rolling out into the distance, the mutinous Shannon flowing on to the sea: all these are to Broderick what central Dublin was to Joyce. Put up by the

Rotary Club at an Athlone hotel, I had a queer feeling on my first visit to the place that I had been there before. It turned out to have been the model for Mrs O'Flaherty Flynn's establishment, the Duke of Clarence, in *The Flood*.

A decade and a half after his death, with reissues of his books, this biography and the Athlone commemoration now a biennial event, his reputation has survived far better than many of his obituarists might have predicted. 'I thought it was over, like a fool. It never is in Ireland,' a character in *The Rose Tree* philosophizes. No, it never is.

D.J. TAYLOR

It is not that I am really cold-hearted:
it is simply that life for me is something in the head,
and almost never in the body.
This is a great fault.

I.

I bake buns

*O*n a visit to Garbally College in the late 1960s John Broderick talked to some young teachers about their work and responsibilities. One of them was moved to ask in turn, 'And what do you do?' 'Ah,' said John, 'What do I do? I bake buns.'

He did, up to a point, bake buns, and was the fourth generation of his family to do so. His great-grandfather Michael was a baker in Athlone from about 1840, and the eldest son, another Michael, took over a bakery in Connaught Street in 1891. It was a period when independent bakeries flourished in towns like Athlone and competition was fierce. Michael's brothers, Francis and Edward, were employed by Newton's, one of the larger rival firms, and all three were involved in legal proceedings. Michael's bake-house was burnt down after a public protest about his continuing the practice of night-work for his employees when other bakeries had abandoned it. He was awarded £75 damages by the court. A few months later his brother Francis was sentenced to a month's hard labour in Tullamore Gaol following a brawl in which a baker from another firm was wounded. Rather than serve the sentence, he fled to America, but became ill in the course of his journey and died a few days after his arrival, in the care of the Sisters of the Congregation of St Joseph. The third brother, Edward, took an action against three others in the bakery trade for insults and death-threats; the three were bound over to keep the peace.

In 1904 Michael went bankrupt. In a wonderfully Irish solution to the problem, he then went off to seek his fortune in America, while his wife Bridget, formerly Bridget Galvin of Clonown, took over what remained of the business and turned it into a profitable concern. Gearoid O'Brien, also a native of Connaught Street and later librarian in Athlone Public Library, refers to Bridget as 'one of the great women of Connaught Street', a group of women who took the places of their lost, failed or strayed husbands and created success out of the initial necessity to support themselves and their families. Her grandson's last two novels, set in a barely disguised Athlone of the 1930s, are filled with women of character, the sort of women who keep the world turning because they know there is no alternative.

Bridget's son John married Mary Kathleen (Mary Kate) Golden from Boyle in 1922, and took over the running of the bakery from his mother. He built it into a major business, supplying towns all over the midlands and west from the base in Connaught Street. John and Mary Kate lived at 5 Connaught Street and their son John Junior was born there in 1924. A previous child,

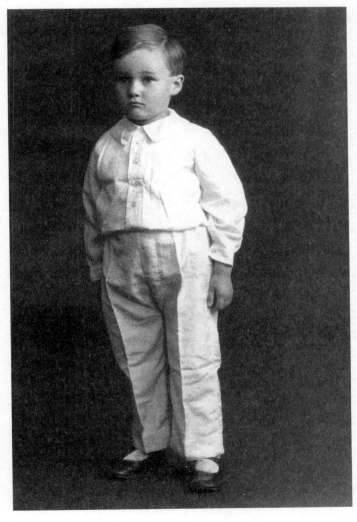

Bernard, had died in infancy, and the safe arrival of John must have given his parents a particular joy. But that joy came to an untimely end three years later in 1927, when John Senior died suddenly, leaving Mary Kate a widow after only five years of marriage, aged twenty-nine and with a three-year-old son. They were to live together until her death in 1974.

John Broderick later recalled his childhood as having been a happy one, but also solitary. His world was Connaught Street, a street of independent small businesses, of which Broderick's Bakery was the most prosperous. Connaught Street is, self-evidently, on the Connaught side of the river Shannon which, at that point, marks the boundary of the ancient provinces of Connaught and Leinster. Young John's first educational experience, with the Sisters of Mercy at St Peter's Infants' School, was positive: the nuns were immensely kind, he never forgot Sister Margaret Mary in particular, and 'while they didn't teach us much except our prayers, and how to count our beads, we had a great time'. It was a gentle start to schooling for a very sheltered only child.

At the age of seven he moved on to the National School, the Dean Kelly Memorial, and found it very different – 'that was the first blow I got in my life' – when he found himself for the first time mixing with boys of all sorts, some of whom 'were determined to make you as tough as they thought they were'. He would have been in any case set apart from his contem-

Dean Kelly Memorial National School; John is in the second row, fifth from the left

poraries by his home situation, and the division was further exacerbated by the fact that his family had money. A school friend of the time tells of John being sought out by other boys because only he had a real leather football, and then being left to stand on the sidelines while they played. There are echoes of that sad little story throughout John Broderick's life, and they do not relate only to material possessions.

He began his secondary education at the Marist Brothers' School, which as he said later took him across the bridge and into a part of Athlone that he knew only slightly, but he had spent less than a year there when the second blow of his life came – a double blow. In 1936 his

mother remarried, and at the same time John was sent away to school.

Mrs Broderick married Paddy Flynn, the manager of her bakery. She was a beautiful 38-year-old woman of some social pretension, not at all in the mould of her mother-in-law, Bridget Galvin. Flynn was a handsome rogue and womanizer, devoted to the business then and thereafter but not likely to slip easily into the role of husband and stepfather. John, who from the age of three had spent almost all his time with his mother, and who had little memory of his father, was now at the age of twelve confronted with her remarriage and with separation from her. It was not unusual at that time for children like him to be sent to boarding-school, but he had already started his secondary schooling, and might have expected to continue it, with the Marist Brothers.

In the event he went first to Summerhill College in Sligo, the diocesan school of Elphin. He had little to say about it in later years except that he found the regime harsh, and he claimed to have been expelled for raiding the kitchen. In January 1938 he was enrolled at St Joseph's College in Garbally, just outside Ballinasloe, and remained there until the end of his formal schooling.

St Joseph's proved to be a happier place. It was the diocesan college of Tuam, housed in a former residence of Lord Clancarty, a classic Anglo-Irish 'Big House', which was spared from burning in the Troubles on condition that it become available as an educational establishment. It was rather less than twenty miles from Athlone, and numbered among its 150 pupils boys of John Broderick's own age from his home town. Although St Joseph's was less austere than Summerhill,

St Joseph's College in Garbally, County Galway
Photo by Michael Geraghty

John again attracted some bullying from classmates, in part for his refusal or inability to conform. His mother was in the habit of despatching lavish hampers to him at school in the family car or in one of the bakery vans, which must also have set him apart from others less fortunate. But when necessary some of the Athlone boys would stand up for him, and his memories of Garbally were not unhappy. The great majority of the teaching staff at the time were priests and several were later mentioned by John Broderick with affection and respect. In particular, Father John Campbell, an English teacher, encouraged his interest in literature and writing, and introduced him to the work of Tolstoy.

Two volumes survive from this time among a collection of books left to the Athlone Public Library in Broderick's will, a copy of Palgrave's *Golden Treasury*, which he used in session 1939–40 and which is covered in the universal schoolboy scribblings of lists of poems to be learned, sonnet rhyme-schemes, an example of a Spenserian stanza and his own name signed several times over with varying flourishes; and a copy of Hilaire Belloc's *Characters of the Reformation*, awarded to John Broderick as first prize for Christian Doctrine.

A significant number of boys from such a college would go on to be priests, or at least to have their vocations tested, and the possibility arose for John Broderick – at this time it was set aside. His mother was notably devout and attended Mass daily throughout her life, but she appears not to have encouraged any

interest he may have shown in the priesthood. Nor indeed did she encourage him to continue his education. He took his Intermediate Certificate and passed it with honours, but left school at seventeen without sitting the Leaving Certificate. In later years he visited the College frequently, and contributed lengthy articles to the College magazine, *The Fountain*. In one such article, printed in 1967, he paid tribute to the 'consideration and understanding' with which he had been treated at the school, and wrote, 'If Catholic education were really as rigid and unfeeling as it is sometimes accused of being, I would either have been expelled or beaten into line. I was a difficult pupil.' It was in the course of some of these later visits that he met Father Cathal Stanley, who then taught English. Father Stanley became a lifelong friend and occasional travelling companion.

The question of what he would do next apparently did not arise. He said later that it was assumed that he would go into the family bakery and in due course take it over, since that was what one did if one's family had a business, and certainly that was his mother's intention. She arranged for him to go to a major bakery company in Dublin to learn the trade, for which he showed little aptitude. Then he was expected to appear in the Connaught Street shop to learn how to deal with commercial travellers and greet customers – for which also he had little aptitude, and which he found awkward and embarrassing.

In one sense, however, his real trade had already begun. By the age of eighteen he had completed what he admitted was an inordinately long novel, never published; more significantly, in these years his ear was attuned to the talk and dealings of Connaught Street and Athlone, which were to be the foundation of his most successful fiction in later years.

Although his apprenticeship at the Dublin bakery was less than successful, the time he spent in Dublin was one of the happier periods of his life. He saw a lot of his great friend Patrick Hunt, a cousin on his mother's side of the family who had spent time at the Brodericks' home in Connaught Street in his early school days, and was very much approved of by Mrs Broderick as a companion for her son. Hunt had married in 1942, and he and his wife frequently went to the theatre and restaurants with John, often accompanied by John's mother; they played bridge together and Patrick and John went riding in Phoenix Park; and John

From left to right: *Annie Golden, Mary Kate, John, and Mary Comerford Hunt at Laytown Strand, 1945*

was godfather to Patrick and Mary's first child.

These were very good days for Broderick's Sunshine Bread (as proof of its established position, mature men in Athlone today recall one of their childhood rhymes: 'Broderick's Bread would kill a man dead / Especially a man with a baldy head'), and Mrs Broderick Flynn shared her taste for travel with her son. They spent time in London and Paris as well as Dublin, and some of John's earliest published writing was to be travel articles for the *Irish Times*. They also shared their appreciation of the very best and smartest clothes and cars – Mrs Broderick Flynn was conspicuously well dressed by the standards of contemporary Athlone, which was not a prosperous town, and photographs of John

Broderick in later years show him in well-tailored tweeds complete with waistcoat and watch-chain, quite the Edwardian gentleman.

None of these pleasures was shared with Paddy Flynn, and indeed nothing in John Broderick's life was ever willingly shared with his stepfather. He implacably rejected the idea of Flynn as his mother's husband and, so far as it was possible under one roof, avoided every kind of contact with him. Mrs Broderick Flynn regarded her son as her natural escort on social occasions in Athlone as much as elsewhere. It is not easy to judge how much of her life was shared with her second husband – there was at least one period of separation that ended in a reconciliation negotiated by a family friend – but he was essential to the running of the business, as was her brother, Harry Golden. At one period in 1944 mother and son were living in Breffni Terrace in Sandycove and at about this time she bought the Bon Bon, an established restaurant in Church Street in Athlone, which she ran successfully for several years. At some time in 1944 or '45 they moved to The Willows, a handsome two-storey bow-windowed house on the canal banks, with a short drive and a large secluded garden.

By now John Broderick had developed a serious interest in books and music, which were to be his two unfailing pleasures throughout his life. He took endless pleasure, too, in the distinctive landscape of the Irish midlands – the great flat expanses of land and water and

The Willows

sky were to be as much a feature of his early novels as the streets and lanes of the small town, and the plot of the last novel he saw published depended on the seasonal flooding along the banks of the river Shannon. From The Willows he would walk his dogs in what were then called the Queen's Meadows. Many years later he recalled an occasion when

I dropped onto my knees to call my little team back to put on their leads. And immediately, the whole scene changed. The flat land which stretches in that area away to the horizon rose and stretched itself tautly against the rim of the sky; and along this rim of the world a couple of greyhounds were racing. For a flashing moment they looked like a bas-relief on an ancient frieze.

Dogs were another constant in his life. Those who interviewed him in later years, whether in Athlone or in

March 1949 – The Geisha, *John Broderick and chorus*

England, would refer to various individuals. In 1976 he had, according to Caroline Walsh, Hector the poodle, Pip the Yorkshire terrier, Buzz the Belgian griffin, Bambi the papillon, and Pug the pug, and in 1987 Mavis Arnold met Hector and Buzz, by then 'his two elderly dogs'. Another of the books now in the possession of Athlone Public Library is a copy of *The Dog Owners' Guide* by Eric Fitch Dalglish, inscribed 'John Broderick Xmas '38', with the endpapers covered in drawings and tracings from the illustrations.

Athlone in the forties, though not prosperous, was not devoid of cultural life. John Broderick, having been involved in school drama at both the Marist Brothers' School and Garbally College, joined the Athlone

Musical Society and Athlone Little Theatre. In the course of 1949 and 1950 he appeared in *The Geisha* and *The Quaker Girl* with the Musical Society, and in *The Shop at Sly Corner* and *Grogan and the Ferret* (a 'rural comedy') in the Little Theatre. He is remembered as having considerable dramatic ability. One fellow per-former recalls, 'He would upstage anybody, but you didn't mind because he was so good and it was all great fun.'

Mrs Broderick Flynn encouraged her son in this kind of social activity. Although he was to say of himself that he was shy and never really a socializer, he clearly found a place in this sort of association; and since his mother was not herself involved, it gave him a context in which to make his own relationships, if only to a limited extent.

He continued to escort his mother to Mass; both beautifully dressed, they would sit always in the same pew at the front of the church. Contemporaries recall that this was not at all a usual practice in Catholic churches, which had never had the English tradition of the 'family pew', and it made the couple quite conspic-uous. The more so as Mrs Broderick Flynn had 'the first mink coat in Athlone'. It is remembered also that on other social occasions, even when his mother was not present, John would in some way be set apart – at a fancy dress party, for instance, he would have an expensive hired costume when 'the rest of us would have things our mothers had thrown together'. By this

stage in his life it cannot be that his mother was actually forcing him into this kind of thing. Nor did she force him into marriage, though there were two or three young women among his social circle in the late forties and fifties of whom she had hopes, and one in particular who realized only much later that Mrs Broderick Flynn had been bitterly disappointed that no match had come of it. They recall him variously: 'I was very fond of him, but I always felt so sorry for him,' and 'I was very fond of him but he could be quite maddening.'

In 1951 there began the John Broderick French connection, about which some questions remain unanswered and many surmises have been made. His habit of inscribing in his books the date (and often the place) at which he bought them shows that in the preceding three or four years he had bought a good deal of French literature, including works by Maupassant, Mauriac, Baudelaire, Gide, Maurois and Green, all in English translations. He went to Paris at this time for an extended period, somewhere between one and two years. It was hardly *la vie de Bohème*, at least in its intention – he went as a *pensionnaire* to a Madame Antoine in the boulevard Bourdon, in the *4e arrondissement*. She was the elderly widow of a judge, and lived with her mother; they kept to a strict daily routine. Broderick was required to be home by eleven o'clock each night, and occasionally he took tea with them in their salon. He continued to buy books, more of Green, Mauriac, Maurois and Gide, now with the addition of Colette, still all in English translation. He admitted later that at this time he was writing 'dozens of novels', over which a fog of oblivion had happily risen so that he could remember nothing about them.

He made a number of acquaintances among both the French and the expatriate literary communities. In interviews he later mentioned various names, and commentators and obituarists were creative in adding others. He certainly knew Julien Green; he certainly never met Gide; he told of meeting Mauriac once and talking briefly about the weather; he regretted that he had not met Colette and did not at all regret that he had not made more of an effort to meet Beckett. He knew Ned Rorem, and was shocked by his drinking habits to the point of remonstrating with him about wasting his talent. He met Gore Vidal, Truman Capote and James Baldwin, all of whom were about his own age: it must have been galling that Vidal, a year younger than Broderick, had already published five novels. He even met grand old Ernest Hemingway, and said he found him 'very nice, very polite'. To be fair to Broderick, he did not in interviews make great claims of close friendships with any of these writers, other than Ned Rorem, but obituarists in particular were to give the impression that he 'settled in Paris' and became part of the literary scene.

When one of his novels was published first in French in 1974, there were some who thought it had been written in French, and one of his closest friends says, 'Of course John would not have been averse to letting people in Athlone believe he wrote it in French!' In fact, it is unlikely that he even looked at the proofs. Commentators also said, almost as a matter of course, that he spoke fluent French, and the desire to learn French may have been one of the reasons for the stay in the boulevard Bourdon. He would not have learnt French in school, and he and his mother would have had little or no need of it when staying in Paris or Cannes. When he was buying French books in Paris he bought them in translation. Among his collection, fewer than a dozen books are in French, and they are without exception copies given to him and inscribed to him by their authors. One of these, a collection of poems by Rochefalmer in a limited edition, has not even had its pages cut. Julien Green mentions in passing

Broderick's lack of curiosity or interest in the books on Green's own bookshelves, and attributes it to the lack of any 'instinct de la culture'. It could just as well have been lack of ease in reading French. His friends in the London book world, while assuming that he spoke the language, on reflection cannot remember ever having heard him do so. He twice inscribed books for Irish friends in French, but in both cases used exactly the phrase used by Green in a book previously given to himself. Nothing, in fact, confirms that he either read or spoke French with ease.

By the beginning of 1953, Broderick was back in Athlone. During his absence his mother had sold The Willows and moved back to Connaught Street, rather to his regret. He had fallen into the habit of writing his address on the flyleaf of his books as 'The Willows, Athlone'. After the return to Connaught Street he wrote only 'Athlone' until their next move took them again to a more salubrious address – it was a characteristic minor vanity.

He was a member of a small committee that in April 1953 organized a tribute to another Athlone native, the tenor John McCormack, who had died some years before. The John McCormack Memorial Concert came within the ambit of the first All-Ireland Drama Festival, and took the form of an address by McCormack's biographer, L.A.G. Strong; a recital of records selected and presented by John Broderick; and a short piano recital by Charles Lynch. Gearoid O'Brien's history of the Festival, in which his own father Brendan was a prime mover, describes a last-minute hitch in the arrangements for the Memorial Concert. After the programme had been printed, L.A.G. Strong became aware that Broderick was proposing to play six Irish songs, five opera extracts, five Leider and art songs, and five 'miscellaneous'. This would have added up to at least one-and-a-half hours of playing time, without allowing for the logistics of changing records, still less for any remarks by the presenter. Strong, it appears, requested Broderick to 'make it a little shorter and less monotonous' and 'eventually Broderick agreed to the cuts'. The story testifies to Broderick's knowledge of the scope of the recordings available, as much as to over-enthusiasm for his own part of a three-man programme. Many of his friends of the time remember spending evenings with him listening to records from his own collection; he had a wide knowledge of singing and singers in particular, and could comment on different interpretations of the same song or aria. Later he presented radio programmes of gramophone recordings for RTÉ, the Irish national broadcasting organization, and whenever he spent time in London he went as often as possible to Covent Garden.

In 1956 came the first of Broderick in print. In September and December of that year the *Irish Times* carried four articles by him, two travel pieces and two book reviews. His account of a performance of *Oedipus* in the ancient theatre at Epidaurus is Broderick of a very good vintage, a detailed critique of the production examining the costumes, the use of the chorus, the projection of the text in the space (with an unfavourable comparison in passing to 'poetry readings in this country') and an understanding of the integration of the whole with the landscape in which the theatre is set and which surrounds both production and audience.

Published two weeks later, an article on 'The Isles of Greece' conveys his sense of the continuity of life in the islands, a synthesis of the antiquities he viewed and the humanity he observed in the Greeks he met in

restaurants and streets. Even at that date he saw the coming danger of mass tourism: later in life he spoke of his thankfulness that he had seen Greece before it was overrun.

In December, in two published columns, he reviewed three books, and clearly the literary editor was well pleased. In the course of the following year, 1957, the paper carried a total of twenty review columns by Broderick, covering thirty-one books. It was a great era of travel-writing: he reviewed James Morris, Walter Starkie, Norman Douglas and Lawrence Durrell, among others, in addition to a number of biographies and collections of memoirs, and one or two volumes of fiction. This represents a fair expenditure of time by the reviewer. He had found a new trade, away from the baking of buns, and he was to practise it throughout the rest of his life: his last review, of Brenda Maddox's biography of Nora Joyce, appeared in the *Irish Independent* in June 1988, just two months before the start of his final illness.

There was a lot of himself in the reviews, in both positive and negative ways. They were informed by his own extremely wide reading, and he could make illuminating comparisons and cross-references between books widely separated in time and subject. Equally, when he reviewed biographies of Maria Callas and Maggie Teyte, he could cite authoritatively occasions when he had heard them sing. He was decisive in his assessments, but not afraid to revisit a writer years later and reassess. He could open out a review into a call-to-arms or a diatribe, especially about matters of the state of Ireland and Irish writing, in a way that was both heartfelt and entertaining. But any of these characteristics could amount at times to self-indulgence. A review of H. Montgomery Hyde's *Oscar Wilde* begins, 'There is nothing new to say about Oscar Wilde, yet people will go on saying it,' and continues with an account of an essay on Wilde by James Agate and a résumé of Broderick's own thoughts on Wilde, which includes references to Sydney Smith, Tibullus, Brendan Behan (much more sensitive and vulnerable than Wilde) and Montaigne. This takes up 80 per cent of the space available for the review: in the remaining 20 per cent he accepts that Montgomery Hyde's work is 'a first-rate biography' and likely to remain the standard one unless somebody of the calibre of Agate should take up the subject. At times it looks as though the percentage of space devoted by Broderick to the actual work under review is in direct proportion to his admiration for it. A review of *Birchwood* hails John Banville as a magician, a genius, the latest in the long and distinguished line of Irish writers who are masters of the English language. The reviewer urges the book on his readers ('it is not easy reading, but it is a most exciting and rewarding experience as all great craftsmanship must be') and persuades them with his account of the plot, the vision, and the comedy of the work. This is all about Banville, and not a word about John Broderick.

Over the thirty years in which he reviewed hundreds of books by Irish, English, French, Italian and Russian writers, among others, there were many consistent notes. As his own novel-writing became established he defended the interests of others. The unavailability of the works of Liam O'Flaherty was 'a disgrace to Ireland', and he castigated the censorship of Francis Stuart and Lee Dunne. He never faltered in his admiration for Kate O'Brien, Jennifer Johnston, Mary Lavin, P.G. Wodehouse, Jane Austen, Françoise Sagan, Colette, Trollope, Henry James; nor in his view that W.B. Yeats was 'an old poseur' who wrote 'sibylline twaddle'. His reviewing of contemporary novels was often didactic, offering guidance to readers and writers alike: he admired John Updike's *Rabbit Redux*, but felt there was 'absolutely no necessity for the scatological language'; readers who dislike *Thérèse Raquin* 'have no real sympathy with the art of fiction'; 'a novelist who has not got genius must write well and with a sense of style'; 'women writing all-male scenes and men all-female scenes are not likely to be successful'; and he was opposed to the whole idea of biographies of writers.

A foolscap notebook in the collection in Athlone Library contains several attempts at the opening paragraphs of a story set in 'Mineret', a town on the Shannon – the notebook is dated 31 July 1949. Clearly he had not given up after the first, 'inordinately long', attempt he had made at eighteen. But his career as a published novelist began in 1961 with a book called *The Pilgrimage*, and a ban.

In 1990 the International Centre on Censorship published a collection of interviews under the title *Banned in Ireland*. Broderick had been interviewed in 1987 and said that at the time of writing *The Pilgrimage* he wrote 'in perfect ignorance of the Censorship Board ... the Censorship Board did not enter my mind'.

The Censorship of Publications Act became law in Ireland in 1929, despite the protests mounted by Yeats, Shaw, George Russell and others. It established the Censorship Board to vet any and all publications circulating within the state and was enthusiastically seconded by activists among the Catholic clergy and laity, notably the

Catholic Truth Society. Zealots scrutinized books for 'indecency' (meaning sex), underlined relevant passages and sent the books to the Board, which frequently recommended banning on the grounds of the underlined sections only, however brief they might be in the context of the whole work. The extreme example was the banning of Kate O'Brien's *The Land of Spices* in 1941 on the grounds of a single sentence. The official banning of a work could lead to an extended effect on any other work by the same author if bookshop owners and librarians, particularly in provincial towns, were put under pressure by the local church. In the early years there was no appeal against the decisions of the Board; the Irish Academy of Letters was founded in 1932 as an attempt to support and protect writers. The Appeal Board was not introduced until 1946, and even thereafter writers had little recourse to it. In the same interview, Broderick was asked whether he had appealed against the banning of *The Pilgrimage* and made it clear why he had not: 'I don't think you can appeal to people who are as stupid and narrow-minded as that ... you would recognise them by appealing, wouldn't you? ... I wouldn't have anything to do with people of that sort.'

In the climate of 1961, it was inevitable that *The Pilgrimage* should be banned. It takes its title from the plan, eventually accomplished, for Michael Glynn, his wife, his nephew who is also his doctor, and his man-servant to join their parish priest on an organized pilgrimage to Lourdes. Glynn is a rich man, but crippled by arthritis and dependent on the care of the servant, Stephen Lydon. Glynn's wife Julia married him before the onset of the illness for the sake of the comfortable social position he could provide – and after the marriage continued the affair she had already begun with her husband's nephew Jim, who introduced the couple. She quickly became aware of her husband's homosexuality, and of his attempt to 'correct' it by the marriage. At the beginning of the novel, Julia receives the first of a series of anonymous letters detailing her own love-making with Jim, and intercepts an identical letter addressed to her husband. Jim takes fright, refuses to continue the affair, and shortly afterwards announces his engagement to a highly suitable girl, the daughter of a senator. Julia, frightened by the letters and deprived of the sexual attentions of Jim, takes Stephen Lydon as her lover, and is appalled when he does in fact fall in love with her. He confides in her his early platonic relationship with a flamboyant Dublin homosexual, and Michael's attempts to initiate an affair with him when he was first employed in the household. Julia further learns that Stephen is in some danger of being involved in the police investigation of the suicide of a young man in the town who has been involved in a homosexual circle in Dublin, and she is able to rescue him from blackmail by giving him the money to buy back incriminating letters.

More than enough in all that for the Catholic Truth Society and the Censorship Board – and none of it accidental. Asked by the interviewer about the Irish attitude to homosexuality, Broderick said, 'I think the Irish are pathological about homosexuality. That was one of the reasons I chose it as the theme for my books, because it never had been done before.'

But as interesting as the 'indecency' charge is the suggestion that the book is, in effect, blasphemous. The accusation was based on the extraordinary final chapter of the book. It consists of a single sentence: 'In this way they set off on their pilgrimage, from which a week later Michael returned completely cured.' The charge is that the man described in the novel could never have been judged worthy of a miraculous intervention by God, but this is a superficial reading of the text.

The preparation of the reader for Glynn's cure begins with the epigraph: 'They that are whole need not the physician: but they that are sick' (Luke 5:31), Christ's justification for his association with publicans and sinners. Michael's marriage to Julia is ascribed to an attempt to 'reform his nature', a consciousness of guilt about his sexuality. In the earliest stages of the planning of the journey he desperately seeks the agreement of Father Victor that, ' "I might walk again. It happens all the time in Lourdes, doesn't it?" ' Later he tells a visiting bishop ' "Lourdes, your lordship ... I have great hopes of that." ' In a rare moment of real contact with his wife he says, ' "Do you think there's any hope of my being cured ... any hope at all?" ' He gets little enough encouragement for his hope. Father Victor, well disposed as he is, cannot summon any words to support him; the bishop 'pursed his lips. The pause which followed was like an icy blast from an open window. "We shall," he murmured at length, "all pray for you, of course." ' Julia believes her husband is deluding himself and is only concerned as to the effect of the inevitable disappointment. But Michael maintains his faith, telling Stephen shortly before they are due to leave for Lourdes,

'I feel that something wonderful is going to happen on this pilgrimage. I have a sort of premonition. Last night I dreamed that I was walking again. Oh, God and his Blessed Mother grant that I will.'

There is no suggestion of hypocrisy in this, he truly believes that a cure is possible and his church clearly teaches that redemption is available to all and faith can move mountains.

Reviewers reacted variously to the use of a single sentence as the final chapter. Some seem to have been more irritated than anything else – one refers to the 'slightly enraged reader' and calls it 'unworthy and unnecessary'. Another describes it as 'supreme irony of situation'. They appear to have suffered a sort of literary shock equivalent to the Catholic shock of readers who imputed blasphemy to the author. Certainly it was no accident on Broderick's part. The whole novel is planned and written with great economy and some elegance. The first paragraph, in seven lines, introduces all the characters and all the essentials of their situation. It shows Stephen outside the closed door of Glynn's bedroom, aware not only of who is inside but of how their chairs are placed and of the subject of their conversation – the pilgrimage. The first chapter, in four-and-a-half pages, effectively delineates the characters and indicates or implies their relationships, their personal rituals, Julia Glynn's risk-taking, Father Victor's innocence, Jim's nervousness. Between this opening scene, which shows the beginning of the pilgrimage project, and the famous final sentence, which shows its conclusion, there are thirty short chapters, none of them extending to more than five or six pages. The progression of the plot is straightforward and most of the writing spare; at the same time the emotional history of each character is conveyed, and their mutual accommodations, deceptions and occasional brutalities are traced. The background is of a claustrophobic small town, seen through Julia's eyes:

Nothing that was not small had ever happened there; nothing of passion, or pride, or reckless emotion. Small change rattled on small wooden counters, and was stored away in little bags ... A little town like all little towns, compounded of petty vices: envy, spite, suspicion, greed.

The Pilgrimage is a fine and assured piece of work with an individual voice. It was published in London by Weidenfeld & Nicolson, in the United States as *The Chameleons*, and in France as *Le Pèlerinage*. In Ireland it was immediately banned, and remained banned until 1975.

Broderick recognized that he was protected from the worst efforts of the zealots by his family's wealth and position as one of the largest employers in Athlone – as he put it, 'If I had been a schoolmaster or a librarian I would never have got away with it.' Others were more vulnerable. In the *Banned in Ireland* interview he mentioned two in particular. John McGahern lost his teaching post in 1965 after the banning of *The Dark* – sacked by the parish priest on the orders of the Archbishop of Dublin, John Charles McQuaid. At the time of that ban, Broderick had written to John Johnson, his London agent, 'Wasn't it awful about John McGahern's book? One might as well be living in Russia. He wrote part of it while he was staying here.' (McGahern's family and Mrs Broderick's were distantly related.) And Broderick believed that the novelist Francis MacManus, who had a disabled child to support, lived in fear of losing his job at Radio Éireann if he wrote freely and fell foul of the Censorship Board.

He was asked too about his family's reaction and was quite categorical:

They didn't respond at all. They said nothing. Nobody belonging to me – my mother, my uncles, my cousins, anyone belonging to me – they never mentioned any of my books to me ever. Not ever. I think it was because they disapproved. Quite apart from anything else, they would disapprove of a writer in the family ... they would think it was a waste of time ... Waste of time. Make much more money baking buns.

This is an extraordinary picture. However little his family shared his literary interests, they can hardly have been unaware of his success. Their complete silence, as he recalls it, must have conveyed something more than disapproval, almost a sort of alienation, as though for them, to write a novel was to go a step too far beyond the journalism he had been writing for some years, in his spare time while baking buns. The community of Athlone and district reacted similarly: 'Nobody ever said anything to me about it.' The attitude of the town, ironically, mirrors the attitudes of the small towns about which he wrote, though Broderick makes an honourable exception of the Longford-Westmeath Public Library Service who, he says, 'certainly did their best to keep *The Pilgrimage* in circulation for those who wanted it until it was unbanned'. In his will Broderick left a number of pictures, records and tapes and some 800 books from his personal collection to the library. But whatever his feelings at the time about the local and national reaction to his first published novel, they must have been balanced to some extent by the response of one of the truly significant names of European literature.

In 1951, while living in Paris, Broderick had introduced himself to the great Julien Green – in the words of Green, 'un jeune inconnu vient sonner à ma porte rue de Varenne'. In the course of that first conversation, Broderick expressed his admiration for Green's most recent novel, *Moïra*, published in 1950, and admitted

Julien Green in his study in the rue de Varenne

that he was a writer himself. They began an occasional correspondence that was to continue for the rest of Broderick's life, and in September 1960 Green received a pre-publication copy of *The Pilgrimage*. He was immediately absorbed by it, and records that he abandoned his own work for two days to read it and reflect on it. He saw at once that it would horrify many readers with its mixture of vice and religion, of inadequate priests and laypeople whose whole spirituality is based on avoiding hell. He concluded also, from the accompanying letter, that the author had little or no idea of what he had achieved in the book, which Green called a masterpiece. That note was to sound throughout the long relationship between these two. In May 1961, by which time *The Pilgrimage* had been published and banned, Broderick visited rue de Varenne again. Green saw in him, ten years after their first meeting, the same openness and the same trace of naïvety – but immediately adds, in his diary account of the meeting, the reflection that Broderick's book is not at all naïve, is indeed 'much more grown-up' than its author. Rereading *The Pilgrimage* in 1974 he notes again that the author is 'even more mysterious than his book', and compares Broderick's awareness of evil with that of Mauriac. And when *The Pilgrimage* was republished in French in 1991, after Broderick's death, Green wrote a preface in which he saw the author as having been moved by an inspiration 'well beyond his years'.

John Broderick's other friends testify to the

importance that he placed on his friendship with Green. At the time of their first meeting Green was already a great figure on the French literary scene, having published fiction, biography, essays and the early volumes of the diaries, which were eventually to cover the years 1926–96. By the time of his first visit to Broderick's home in Athlone in 1974, he had been elected to the Académie Française in the place of François Mauriac. He knew everyone – the literary figures of France, England and America as a matter of course, but also the great names of the social and artistic scene and of the Catholic clergy and laity – he read everything, he travelled everywhere, and he recorded it all in the diaries, which testify also to his spirituality and his constant questioning of his own relationship with good and evil. Green was to reproach himself later for his own failure to realize how important the friendship was to Broderick. He continued to be bemused by the apparent discrepancy between the John Broderick he came to know over the years and the mysterious power of his writing, in particular what he calls the 'vélocité' of *The Pilgrimage*, which he thought missing from the later novels. He believed that Broderick would have made a greater literary reputation for himself had he lived in London or New York, though it is not clear whether he implies that the effect would have been on Broderick's writing or on its recognition by readers and critics. But whatever he later became, or failed to become, *The Pilgrimage* announced Broderick as a novelist.

❦

Three novels appeared in the next four years – *The Fugitives* in 1962, *Don Juaneen* in 1963 and *The Waking of Willie Ryan* in 1965. Elements of *The Pilgrimage* recur in varying proportions – the small-town setting, the church rituals, a variety of priests, sex without love and often without pleasure, and humour in minute observation and in wonderful set pieces.

The Fugitives is set in an unnamed small town, a midland town on a river, its market-place dominated by 'the huge grey battlements of the old castle of King John', its hinterland 'the huge flat expanse' of a turf-bog – Athlone to the letter. Lily Fallon, stepdaughter of the owner of Fallon's Select Bar and General Grocery, arrives back in the town from London expecting to see her brother Paddy, also returned from London. Paddy, however, finds himself on the run from the police after the assassination of an under-secretary for Northern Ireland by the IRA and is followed: first by his IRA minder Hugh Ward, and in due course by the police of England and Ireland. Ward exercises a sinister influence on both brother and sister, something compounded in both cases of sex and sadism, authority and menace. Hetty Fallon, Lily's widowed stepmother, is kept in ignorance as long as possible: the watchful town and the gardaí are led to believe that Ward has come in pursuit of Lily. But Paddy gradually cracks under the strain and, when they hear that one of the associates in the murder has been arrested in England, Ward, Lily and Paddy hide out in a cabin on the bog, where they are found by the pursuing English police and Paddy is shot dead with Ward's gun.

There are few glimpses of the Church and its priests in this story, but there are both convictions and rituals. Paddy expresses his devotion to the IRA, known to him as 'the Organisation', in terms of his readiness for self-sacrifice, atonement, in order that 'something will be achieved' and that others too will be prepared to die. Hetty's sister-in-law, 'Aunt Kate', who recognizes in Paddy that distortion of the religion in which he was brought up, is herself a professed atheist, but lives in a bare room like a convent cell and looks 'like an old nun who has taken off the veil'.

And the narrative is punctuated five times by descriptions of Mrs Fallon's meetings with her friend Mrs Lagan, introduced on the first occasion by the words, 'It was a ritual.' The first enactment forms the whole of Chapter 5. Mrs Lagan arrives in the shop as though by chance.

'Oh, there you are, Mrs Fallon. I was just passing. I thought I'd drop in for a moment.'

'Come in here and sit down,' said Hetty, reciting her part of the antiphon.

'I've just finished my rosary.'

'The Sorrowful Mysteries today,' said Mrs Lagan, edging

her way into the 'snug'. This part of the ritual varied with the day. On Mondays and during Advent the Joyful Mysteries, on Fridays and during Lent the Sorrowful Mysteries. The mulled port was already waiting on the table with one Digestive biscuit beside each glass.

The opening responses of the liturgy continue with remarks on fish, this being Friday. Then the port is addressed.

They raised their glasses.

'In the honour of God.'

'A lovely drop of port, thank God,' said Mrs Lagan, wiping her mouth delicately with the corner of a lace hand-kerchief.

'It will do you good,' said Hetty, shifting heavily in her seat and looking at Mrs Lagan with half-closed eyes. 'You look a bit pale.'

Mrs Lagan closed her eyes and slumped in her chair, letting her hands fall by her side in a gesture of complete exhaustion. 'I don't know what way I am,' she said in a weak voice. 'I feel completely washed out. Not a wink of sleep last night, sitting up every ten minutes sprinkling holy water over the poor souls in Purgatory, and then dragging myself out for eight o'clock Mass. I feel I could drop down and die.'

'Terrible sudden times,' said Hetty, shaking her head. 'Nothing but people dropping dead all over the place. I'd go to bed for a few days if I were you, your lips are very blue. Mrs Sheridan was the very same. In here getting her groceries one minute and stone dead on the bridge ten minutes later. But I noticed her lips. Blue.' She sipped her port contentedly.

Mrs Lagan recovers her ground with some aspersions on the state of her friend's business, but Mrs Fallon moves on to the next stage.

'Have you heard from Peter lately?' she asked gruffly.

Mrs Lagan stirred uneasily in her chair. Her only son had gone to Australia some years before, and everyone knew that he had never written to her since.

'Oh, yes,' she said brightly, tapping her glass angrily with her nail. 'The usual letter, you know. Going on well.'

'It's a wonder he never comes home,' said Hetty inexorably.

'Business, you know. He has such a terrible lot to do. Of course he's always writing for me to go out, but I'm too old to settle in a new country. Besides, Ireland is the best place. Thanks be to God for one place where God and his Blessed Mother are given their due. Not like England.'

'Or Australia.' Hetty sipped her port contentedly.

'I see you have Lily home,' countered Mrs Lagan. 'Poor girl, she looks washed out. Is she sick?'

'No,' replied Hetty shortly. 'Is that a new blouse you have on?'

Mrs Lagan was not to be put off. She patted her blouse and crossed her legs, a daring gesture, made only when she felt she was really going to discomfort her old friend.

'I've had this blouse for ages. A really good thing never wears out, or goes out of fashion. Did Lily bring you home any clothes from England?'

'I don't need any clothes,' said Hetty angrily.

'I suppose she's on holiday, poor girl,' went on Mrs Lagan with a pitying smile. 'What is she working at now?'

'She's a supervisor.'

'All those supervisors,' hooted Mrs Lagan. 'London is full of them, all Irish.'

'I suppose it's the same in Australia. What does Peter say?'

'Peter has his own business. He employs several supervisors.'

And so the ritual continues until the final act, when Mrs Lagan gives Mrs Fallon a sixpence for the Foreign Missions box, and receives in exchange a sixpence for the weekly raffle for the new parochial house. The cumulative effect of the repetitions and variations in the dialogue between the two old women prepares the way for the fifth and final enactment to form the last chapter, set a year after Paddy's death, clarifying the aftermath of the earlier events, and allowing Broderick to end the novel with just six or seven lines of compassion for brave, bereaved Mrs Fallon.

In terms of narrative skill, plotting and characterization, this is a second fine novel, appearing just a year after *The Pilgrimage*. The background to the action is broader than the single household of the Glynns, and the ending is dark and dramatic. The reviewer in the *Times Literary Supplement* wrote,

This is admirably economical and to the point ... The writing is taut and controlled, and the characters of the hunted gunman and his sister both unusual and completely convincing.

Kate O'Brien said of him,

[He] explores frustrated life, soured ideals and the pattern of dark religions and anti-religious stupidity in an Irish town ... he throws a light of truth and understanding into very dark holes in the Irish spirit ... he is one determined and melancholy kind of realist.

Her picture of Broderick's work at this early stage of his career is dark, and she could not foresee the ways in which his writing would evolve, but already she was prepared to say, 'He is a master of form.'

Don Juaneen is a lighter dish, leavened with humour, love and innocence, even though it ends in the classic situation of a very young girl (Caroline) leaving Ireland to have her illegitimate baby in England. At least she has loved the man who has made her pregnant, and she has the love of her father who grieves for her and for his own inability to help her.

The setting is the suburbs of Dublin, but John Quill, Caroline's father, and Philip O'Connor, her lover, were schoolboys together in 'a country town in the midlands', and John married Sybil, Caroline's mother, after meeting her in Dublin at a Sacred Heart sodality dance and walking her home 'when he discovered that she came from the same small town in the midlands as himself'. O'Connor is rich and successful, from a family who had owned a chain of drapery shops; Quill is a minor official in a government department, always short of money and from time to time forced to borrow from O'Connor, in an adult echo of their unequal childhood relationship. Sybil Quill has pretensions to gentility, based on a small legacy, which has long since disappeared; O'Connor's wife, Lilian, is a sophisticated English woman.

John Quill moves in a circle as restricted as any small town – going to his office, meeting his friend Paul Shine at Mick's Lounge, driving with his wife and daughter to Vico Road on Sundays to park the car overlooking Killiney Bay and sit, windows closed, to read the papers. He nurtures a wholly false reputation among his fellow-drinkers as a womanizer, but is shocked by the suggestion that Paul, who makes a living as promoter of the sweeps and raffles run by various religious orders, may collect more than money from the women he visits weekly. Paul keeps him informed about the financial aspects – the summer is a bad time,

'... everybody is saving up for the holidays. Mother of Virtues is still all right, the prize money is so big they can't resist it, and the Tomb of the Apostles is fair. But Blessed Mary Magda O'Hara is gone to hell ... the competition is awful. It was all right until the Jesuits started.'

The arrival of Paul's niece from across the water involves innocent John Quill in a variety of entertaining situations, which almost force him to desert Mick's Lounge for the Green Bar, where women do not go and where there is a much higher class of graffiti in the

Gents. Sybil accepts her husband's drinking as an entirely appropriate thing for a husband to do, and is happy with her terrace house because it has a window on either side of the front door. She is happy also that their daughter goes to the Protestant tennis club, since even if Church of Ireland members have little hope of getting to heaven, 'she was equally convinced that they were socially superior, more honest and more reliable than her Catholic neighbours'.

But poor, snobbish Sybil is all too easily drawn into the web of Miss Rose Blake, who destroys her tranquillity by telling her about her daughter's affair with O'Connor, under the pretence of acting as a friend 'because sooner or later you'd hear it from somebody else. They'd tell you out of spite, just to watch your face.' Miss Blake has been greatly disappointed by missing the opportunity to break the same news to Lilian O'Connor, another of her friends. The fact of the affair is brutally presented to John Quill by his wife, and is instantly rejected by him as impossible, no more than a piece of malicious gossip, but he has to accept it in time, grieving for his daughter: 'Mr Quill had been ill-prepared for life by his parents. They had been too happy.' Sybil, grieving in her own way, 'had felt like going to Mass every morning; but to do so when it was not her habit would, she knew, in her own town, have prepared the neighbours for imminent calamity', so she dare not do more than slip into the church to light candles. It is Sybil who knows what has to be done for Caroline, whatever her own feelings; and John who, after his daughter has gone, walks in misery down to the seafront at Dun Laoghaire every day to see the mail-boat sail and feel the harsh reality of modern Ireland overshadowing the great heroic past.

That final picture in the last chapter of the book is a risky business, showing Quill against a historical background in which Broderick invokes the Norsemen, Dermot and O'Brien, Henry and Bruce and Silken Thomas, Fitzgerald and Tone, O'Connell and Pearse and Joyce, but it is short enough and anchored enough to be easily accepted by the reader. Less so are the interventions of the authorial voice dispensing sentences such as, 'Like all women she accepted bad news quicker than good,' and 'Love is renounced in a multitude of ways.' This had started in *The Fugitives* – 'those who have pulled up their roots have nothing but bleeding stumps with which to explore the no-man's-land they inhabit'. Where were the editors when they were needed? A later editor recalls that Broderick hated to correct or revisit anything he had written, complained bitterly that galley proofs were too big for his writing table, and refused to consider using a larger table. One of his friends conjured up a picture of John, faced with an editor's suggestion, 'taking a twirl about the room and disappearing', and he wrote to another friend as an excuse for some delay,

I was correcting proofs, or rather galleys, which is really hard labour, and should be the sort of thing educated prisoners in Mountjoy are encouraged to do. It absorbs all one's energies, so that one can think of nothing else, and leaves one fit only for falling into bed as early as one can: surely an ideal prison situation.

Unchecked, the authorial intrusions were to become something of a weakness in later years; at this early stage it is no more than an occasional flaw, surprising because of the quality of the writing in other respects.

Broderick found another new balance for his fourth novel, *The Waking of Willie Ryan*, published in 1965. He returns to 'the great central plain of Ireland', to a small town on whose outskirts in winter 'the mighty Shannon overflowed its banks for a mile on either side'. Michael and Mary Ryan live outside the town in an ugly Victorian villa with stone lions outside the front door, coach lamps and a stone gorgon's head affixed to the front wall, a stag's head and an oil painting of Pope Pius XII in the hall, Crown Derby, sugar-tongs and ormolu clocks in the drawing-room – all this splendour proceeding from the profits of Kieran McDonogh & Co Ltd, Wholesale and Retail Grocers, Wine Merchants, Coal Importers and General Hauliers, and the efforts therein of Mrs Ryan, née McDonogh. This is the first of Broderick's pictures of the rising Catholic, moneyed bourgeoisie, evoked in their possessions. Mary Ryan and her friend Kitty Carroll meet for worship in Mrs Ryan's drawing-room:

Rings were flashed and examined; hair was patted, and the skills of the various Dublin coiffeurs commented upon. Kitty kneaded her jawline with stumpy fingers and gave the name of a new cream; Mary responded with the address of a corset-maker in Curzon Street. Side by side they moved about the stifling room, fingering silver, stroking satin and velvet ... comparing consecrated possessions in low tremulous voices ... in silent communion before a riotous whirl of colour by Jack B. Yeats, bought for a song fifteen years before, framed in gold leaf, and now representing a profit of two hundred per cent. They ... admired again their own rich vestments: symbols of an ancient faith, whose abundant graces were made manifest to all in their persons and their homes.

This extract was referred to years later by Broderick in a letter to Patrick Murray – 'I think on the whole [*The Waking of Willie Ryan*] is my best book. I must say I am rather proud of chapter 4, part 2. It hits several nails on heads and is fun too.' Broderick was part of the moneyed Catholic bourgeoisie himself – his mother had a drawing-room and he enjoyed living in fine houses, but for all that, the theme was deliberately pursued. In a discussion on the future of the Irish novel, printed in the *Irish Times* in 1970, he said, 'I think the future of the Irish novel is the examination of the little grocer's republic which we have set up since the treaty, with its petty bourgeois snob-bishness, hypocrisies and pretensions.' In *The Waking of Willie Ryan* the theme is lightly treated, and is indeed fun, but it also illuminates the real drama of the narrative.

At the outset of the novel, Willie Ryan, brother of Michael, arrives back in his home town having escaped from the asylum where he has been incarcerated, and unvisited, by his devout Catholic family for twenty-five years. The ostensible reason for the incarceration was an attack on his sister-in-law: the real reason, his affair with a young man who introduced him to the pleasures of literature, music and art, but also to his own hedonistic circle. Mary Ryan, and through her the rest of the town, is confirmed in the belief that the banishment was justified by the much-repeated fact that in all the years in the asylum he has steadfastly refused to go to confession or attend Mass – has failed to 'attend to his duties', unlike his pious relatives and fellow-citizens.

But to the reader Willie is an appealing, admirable character. He knows himself and therefore sees clearly what is going on in other people; he can tolerate hypocrisy in others while having not a trace of it himself; he sees the way in which people are trapped in patterns and cycles, while believing themselves to be free; he recognizes how easily devotion to the Church can replace personal moral choices. When he knows he is about to die, he goes along with the extraordinary family ceremony of a private Mass. He is prepared to conceal the fact that he has not been to confession in preparation – conceal it, that is, from everybody except the priest, to whom he reveals it after the event, and who is satisfactorily shaken out of his complacency. Through Willie the reader is also shown other characters – his brother

Michael, filled with shame and remorse but quite unable to express it; his nephew Chris, too tied to the piety of his family to accept the new freedom offered by Susan Carroll; the excellent asylum nurse Halloran, as perceptive as Willie himself and less gentle; and Father Mannix, who was complicit in 'putting away' Willie in the first place.

All these, and others, are satisfyingly complete and convincing pictures, and the action unrolls in Broderick's characteristic short chapters. Most of the development of the action comes through the dialogue, always Broderick's greatest gift and displayed here with particular skill.

Along the way there is a lot more fun to be had too. Miss Pinkie White, who writes poetry, and Mrs O'Neill, who paints watercolours for the nuns' bazaars, offer an occasional commentary on people and events in an echo of Hetty Fallon and Mrs Lagan in *The Fugitives*. The description of the Mass held in Chris Ryan's house occupies four chapters. The first begins with the sentence, 'Ritual took over and kept them from thinking': the ritual is the preparation of tablecloths, glass, cutlery and food. The next chapter opens, 'Ritual which ordains the outward gesture cannot always prevent accidents or bickering': Chris breaks his wrist, Michael has a fall, the chimney cannot be prevented from smoking. Next, 'And then it began to rain,' and next, the day of the Mass itself, 'Next day it was still raining,' so that starched linen drooped and walls were streaked with moisture. The ceremony of the Mass is described with all Broderick's knowledge and reverence for the Latin text, the vestments, vessels and gestures – balanced by the description of the five-course meal that all present consume immediately afterwards, at ten o'clock in the morning: melon, soup, fish, chicken, trifle, Monrachet, port and brandy. And so the next chapter begins, ' "The Mass went off very well," said Willie,' and develops into Willie's confrontation with Father Mannix, which is the pivot of the whole narrative.

The Waking of Willie Ryan was recognized by reviewers as a significant step in Broderick's progress as a novelist. The serious treatment of the theme that observance does not indicate spiritual understanding and that conformity is no guarantee of moral integrity was united to his already established gifts of character-ization, dialogue, humour, exuberance of language and narrative skill. In just four years he had had four novels published in England and the United States and two in France. The promise of *The Pilgrimage* was being fulfilled and the writer had found his path. Buns could well be baked without him.

II.

A sentient mess

*O*ne of the most interesting items in Athlone Public Library's Broderick collection is a spiral-bound 'Waverley Student's Notebook' in which Broderick made notes of ideas for novels, plays and short stories. The earliest dated entries are for June 1963, but eight pages have been removed from the front of the notebook so that it now starts at page 9. In all there are over a hundred closely written pages, occasionally dated at the time of writing or later, and the final entry is marked 'Bath, 1st Nov, 1987'. There are sixty-five ideas or outlines, some little more than a line or two, some extending over several pages. Some of the published novels have their origins here: the plot of *The Flood*, published 1987, is recognizable in an entry made somewhere between 1963 and 1965, which includes the names of two of the characters used in the final version. There are also early ideas for *The Pride of Summer*,

Photo by Michael Geraghty

London Irish, *A Prayer for Fair Weather* and *The Rose Tree*. In the pages covering the first two or three years of the notebook there are outlines of eight plays, one of them *The Enemies of Rome*.

Among the ideas that never came to fruition, or at least not to publication, are many that are quite fascinatingly suggestive. In 1982, the year in which *The Trial of Father Dillingham* appeared, he wrote this outline for a novel:

the famous atheist whose mistress finds after his death an intimate journal he kept of his relationship with God. All the unexplained absences in his life were visits to priests. God is the really [taboo? illegible] factor in modern life – everyone is ashamed of admitting to him.

That is a subject worthy of Mauriac, if ever there was one, and *The Trial of Father Dillingham* suggests that Broderick could have made a fine novel of it. The title 'An evening in Ravenna' appears, attached first to an outline plot involving a young Irishman in Ravenna. An unpublished and undated short story with this title, not a development of the outline, has Ravenna only as the setting in which an elderly man tells a young Irishman a story of lost love – it is a good story, but had Somerset Maugham written it the title could as well have been 'An evening in Rangoon'. (Later in the notebook the title is used for a possible variation of the Narcissus/ Echo myth, and years later Broderick was still referring in articles and interviews to 'a novel set in Ravenna, which obsesses me'.) Another, more detailed outline with the note 'use title with Vienna in it', involves a matriarch and her son ('a clear case of mother-fixation'), his friend ('breezy, handsome, outdoor-type, passionate') and the matriarch's elder daughter, who is secretly in love with the highly unsuitable manager of the family business who is markedly of the same type and temperament as her father. There is a possible novel to be called 'The last goods train', the story of a young boy brought up by two maternal aunts in 'a street like Connaught St', the boy 'a chameleon', adapting himself to other people in his desire to please.

One or two ideas may have seemed like fantasies at the time but now appear quite credible: a play about the marketing for huge profit of bottled air purporting to come from Brighton, Cannes or Florida, and a story about tins of food in a supermarket into which poison has been introduced by a small shopkeeper put out of business by the big chain. There are notes in the final three years for what he refers to as 'Bath stories' and a list of names taken from the *Daily Telegraph* death-notices as being suitable for the Bath setting. In the last pages the handwriting is increasingly shaky and in parts illegible, but the final entry is discernibly the outline of a story to be set in 'Bridgeford' and involving an incomer attempting to buy up an orchard.

Throughout the notebook jottings occur also on technical possibilities: 'a novel in which the characters have no communication with one another at all, except through Things'; 'a spy story reflected in the minds of two women: husbands spies'; 'story told entirely in feelings, sensations, no dialogue'; 'story entirely in dialogue'. They testify to Broderick's preoccupation with what he referred to variously as his trade or his craft. More than once he drew an analogy with singing:

People have this idea that all you have to do is sit down and dash off a novel; they don't realise that you've got to learn your craft the same as any other person. It's like having a singing voice – it still has to be trained.

In 1969 he gave a lecture on 'The novel', which was afterwards printed in *The Fountain*, the magazine of Garbally College, and continued the theme:

Most writers are born with a feeling for words, an instinct for them, and this is certainly something which cannot be acquired. But it must be refined by hard practice, and the wearying task of trial and error ... And you must do it alone; no-one can really help you.

The lecture dwells more on the novelist than the novel, the storyteller whose task remains, whatever changes there may be in the world around him, and indeed whatever contradictions there may be within him.

If you are one of those people who like others to be direct, simple and uncomplicated I would advise you to keep away from writers because from your point of view they are nothing more than a mess. But they are a sentient mess; and sometimes although not always – it is not necessary for a novelist at all – intelligent as well.

His devotion to the craft informed his criticism as well. He recognized the master-craftsmen, and was generous both in print and in life to young writers in whom he saw promise of equal devotion. At the same time he did not spare those who, to his eye, were primarily interested in commercial success and public acclaim.

The Waverley Notebook is in a sense the most personal document Broderick left behind, an intimate account of the years in which writing was the most important thing in his life. It was not shared with anybody, not intended for publication, never mentioned in his interviews, which were so often preoccupied with things much less important. And yet, for all the importance to him of writing, those who read *The Waking of Willie Ryan* in 1965 and looked forward to his next novel were to have a long wait. The next novel did not appear until 1973.

Early in 1972 he wrote to John Johnson, who had been his agent since the early sixties, 'I am feeling much better after five years of non-drinking, but I will never forget the first two – the drying-out process was pretty grim.' As a young man he had not drunk alcohol at all, even in the years in Paris, and he said later that he had not started until he was in his thirties, '... but I've made up for it since'. By 1964–5 he was drinking so heavily that his doctors told him that unless he stopped he would die, probably of a heart attack. He was quite clear about his reason for starting.

I was never really a socialiser, I was always very shy. When I was drinking it did give me extra Dutch courage ...

I don't even like drink particularly, but I like what it does for me ... I'm a very shy person, I have to force myself to meet people. Drink offers a release from social strictures.

These were years when the success of the early novels necessarily brought him into contact with publishers, editors, reviewers and others away from his Athlone setting and into a sort of 'public' life that his family, even his mother, refused to acknowledge. That enforced socializing may have been enough to make him resort to alcohol to ease the strain.

But the need for Dutch courage to overcome shyness must have arisen also in connection with his sexuality. Patrick and Mary Hunt, with whom he shared happy times when he was first in Dublin, became aware that he was changing in some way. In retrospect they pinpointed the turning-point in their friendship as 1946–7, when John gradually lost what Patrick calls 'his natural sunshine and spontaneity' and 'seemed to be hiding something'. That something may have been the realization of his homosexual orientation as he reached his early twenties.

Many of those with whom he mixed in Paris were openly homosexual. Julien Green, whom he so much admired, was then in his fifties and had a lifestyle in which the people closest to him were his lifelong partner, the diplomatic journalist Robert de Saint-Jean; Green's adopted son, Eric Jourdan; and his sister, Anne, who lived with Green and Eric and translated a number of his books into English as well as producing at least one novel herself. Green admitted in his diaries that he continued to seek out anonymous sexual encounters long after his relationship with de Saint-Jean was established and openly recognized.

Among the men of his own age whom Broderick knew in Paris, Gore Vidal was flamboyantly homosexual and, like other Americans in the group, had come to Paris in search of sexual freedom, writing about 'brief

anonymous adhesions'. Patrick Hunt, who was familiar
with the sort of school that Broderick had attended,
assumed that a boy of John's obviously soft, rather
spoiled nature, who refused to conform to the rugby-
playing philistine norms, would inevitably have been
the object of sexual attentions in his teenage years. A
brief entry in the Waverley Notebook, undated but
headed 'Autobiography', includes the single line 'Summerhill. Night in cubicles, Garbally', but the terms in
which he wrote of his time at Garbally seem to refute
any suggestion of sexual violence or abuse.

Those who knew him later and assumed that his
orientation was homosexual quote no evidence of any
sustained relationship at any time of his life. When he
was being interviewed in connection with his novels,
the question of his sexuality occasionally arose and
was dealt with fairly evasively, as a matter that it was
inappropriate to discuss, not least because of the
embarrassment it might cause to his family. He was
quoted in one such interview as saying, 'I think that
most men are bi-sexual – as are most women,' the sort
of gnomic utterance that was typical of his public pro-
nouncements on private matters. The predominance in
his novels of loveless, unhappy sex has attracted the
accusation of misogyny. It may imply no more than a
fear of or distaste for sex. Of the only two examples in
his work of close and loving sexual partnerships, one is
homosexual and the other heterosexual. In two of the
early novels he shows a young man taken up by a

sophisticated older man who opens up to him the world of culture and intellect – in each case the relationship is recalled as something idyllic, unforgettable and unrepeatable, in which sex, if it occurred at all, was unimportant. The poet Desmond Egan quotes a letter from John Broderick in 1965 in which he admits to being over-analytical. ' "It is not that I am really cold-hearted: it is simply that life for me is something in the head, and almost never in the body. This is a great fault." ' Whether it is a fault, a curse or a blessing, it is an attitude to life that conduces to isolation, and along with confusion or doubt or unhappiness about his sexuality, it can only have added to his unease in social situations and increased the temptation to resort to alcohol.

At one point, talking about the 'drinking years', he said, 'Every family has someone with a drink problem.' Patrick Hunt recalls that John Broderick's father was a drinker and that Mrs Broderick had suspected that her husband's drinking was abnormal. Hunt's father, an occasional drinking companion, accepted that John's father did 'kill himself drinking' and that 'young John will kill himself just as his father did', so there may well have been an inherited tendency towards alcoholism. Whatever the source or the stimulus, alcoholism certainly took over in these years and remained a threat for the rest of his life. He wrote about it once, passionately. In May 1973 he reviewed *Paddy Maguire is Dead*, a novel by Lee Dunne banned by the Censorship Board. Broderick's diatribe against the Board, such as he never wrote in defence of his own books, is based on two questions:

Do the censors know what they are doing? And in particular do they know what this novel is all about? If they do, then they are a truly sinister body, and if they do not, they are an ignorant and arrogant bunch who have once again made the Republic of Ireland ridiculous.

For the novel is about alcoholism: 'Every incident, every character, every act of the anti-hero Maguire, is motivated and overshadowed by the effects of this dreadful disease'; 'it reveals exactly and honestly what it is really like to be an alcoholic'. Maguire

suffers from black-outs whenever he drinks. His sexual exploits are of a 'special nature' because they are not the actions of a responsible man. The desperation, the loneliness, the craving for affection and the wild pursuit of it, are characteristics of this disease, and are instantly recognisable to anyone who has any experience of it ...

Do [the members of the Censorship Board] know anything of alcoholism? If they do, and then quite deliberately suppress this book, then God forgive them. If they don't, it is about time they learned. Because at the end Lee Dunne indicates how this disease can be arrested, although it cannot be cured ... if they are really ignorant of the effects of alcoholism as a disease, I know of many people who would be only too happy to explain it to them.

There is no mistaking the rage in this review, and no

mistaking the truth of its description of the state of mind of the alcoholic.

Broderick, in the grip of the disease, could be an embarrassment. He was on occasion 'banned' from various pubs and bars in Athlone; a friend of the time says that there were spells when he was 'just the town drunk' who would roam around the town at night looking for anybody who would drink with him; another friend recalls having to wait outside the Brodericks' house until he could see that Mrs Broderick had gone upstairs to bed, and only then going in with a bottle of gin. At some point Broderick joined Alcoholics Anonymous, and was more than once accompanied to its meetings by Lee Dunne. These are unhappy pictures to find coinciding with the years when he was enjoying the successful publication of four novels, some twenty years after he had written his first. In 1962 he and his mother and stepfather had moved out of Connaught Street to The Moorings, a very large nineteenth-century house on the outskirts of Athlone, originally built by a retired naval officer with his prize money from the Napoleonic Wars. The house had about twenty rooms and extensive grounds, and would have been a fine background for continuing literary success; less so as a background for 'the drinking years'.

With or without drink, there could be a great deal of embarrassment and irritation for those around John Broderick. He had little sense of the effects of his actions on others in social circumstances – he would

The Moorings

arrive at people's homes at inconvenient times, sometimes in a highly inappropriate state, and stay until he
had to be either put out or escorted home. He expected
a good deal of attention from friends who had more
immediate calls on their time and could take offence if
it was not forthcoming, and he could be capricious in
his friendships. He would take people up for a time and
then drop them without explanation, even getting his
housekeeper to turn them away at the door, and a few
months later would expect to renew the friendship
without any explanation of the breach.

At times it suited him for some reason to represent
himself as 'an Athlone businessman' – the idea is still
greeted with snorts of derision by real Athlone businessmen who could never take seriously the picture of
Broderick as one of their company. One of the most

successful of them describes his behaviour as 'all that eejiting-about' and quotes as an example an occasion when Broderick, recently returned from a holiday in Morocco, turned up 'in black leather, carrying a hand-bag'. A former employee of the bakery recalls that on occasion Broderick would put in an appearance there as though to assert that he, and not Paddy Flynn, was in charge.

Many in Athlone knew little of him as a writer, having at best read a few pages of one of his novels, and knew nothing of his generosity in encouraging younger writers in whom he saw aspirations that reached out beyond the immediate scene. Gearoid O'Brien recalls Broderick, a friend of his parents, helping him with his study of *Wuthering Heights*, a set text for the Leaving Certificate, and agreeing to give a lecture to other exam candidates. He also writes of Broderick's generosity with 'his time, his praise, his advice and his books' when O'Brien began to have poems accepted for publication. Patrick Lawrence, who as a young man was introduced to Broderick by Adam Lamb, a Church of Ireland priest, has similar memories of generosity. Both O'Brien and Lawrence have made two points about the novelist: that they sensed in him a lonely, unhappy man, and that they never in the time they spent with him had the slightest unease or embarrassment arising from his sexuality.

In those drinking years even the stream of reviewing dried up – no columns appeared between August 1964

Taken from the 1964 Obolensky edition of The Fugitives

and December 1965. In 1966 there were to be fifteen reviews for the *Irish Times*, and thereafter there were some in every year. Meanwhile Broderick's agent was dealing with a variety of matters concerning the novels: there was a good deal of correspondence with Ivan Obolensky of New York who, when under contract as agent for the distribution of the novels in the United States, began publishing hardback editions under his own imprint without any consultation or financial agreement; in 1966 Amicus Productions at Shepperton enquired about the possibility of a film version of *Don Juaneen*; and in 1967 a request was received from C.V. Ganesan M.Sc., a student in Mysore, for permission to translate *Don Juaneen* into Malayalam (this was refused). In 1968 Broderick was elected to membership of the Irish Academy of Letters, but in the same year Weidenfeld & Nicolson rejected *The Trial of Father Dillingham*, and in 1969 Faber turned down 'The love front.'

In 1970 the *Irish Times* printed a discussion on the future of the Irish novel featuring Terence de Vere White, Kevin Casey, Richard Power and John Broderick. In the course of it, Broderick talked of 'a novel that I would like to write, a large novel which would bring my home town and its various strata of people to life in universal terms'. In January 1971 a series of three Broderick articles in the *Irish Times* gave advice on 'How to succeed in literature without really trying'. The first option was not to write anything, but to become the author of the 'great unwritten masterpiece' and to talk a lot about it in Dublin pubs. The second, to tape and transcribe hours of people talking about themselves, preferably in the country, or to rehash a previous biography and throw in a few new photographs or family letters; either method would create a 'bookject' that could hardly fail to win acclaim. The third, to abandon grammar and coherence and concentrate on obscurity and 'flow', and at least someone would get a Guggenheim scholarship to elucidate the result. Clearly the Broderick spirit was coming back, and he did not like what he saw around him ('bookject' is an invaluable coinage). After the worst of the drying-out years were over, he had resumed travelling: in 1970–1 he had been to Morocco, Oslo, Copenhagen and Paris. And now at last his latest novel had been accepted and was about to appear.

'The love front', rejected by Faber in 1969, appeared as *An Apology for Roses*, published in 1973 by Calder and Boyars. Shortly before the publication date, Broderick had written to John Johnson about the necessity for advertising to ensure success – 'Have you heard that Edna O'Brien is going to strip naked on the London stage? What do you suggest I should do, short of this?' No such sacrifice was needed. The book was an instant bestseller. Thirty thousand copies were sold within eight days: extracts were printed in *Hibernia* and the *Irish Times* in the week of publication; within a year the paperback edition came out from Pan, and much to Broderick's amusement was seized by the Customs and Excise in Dublin for submission to the Censorship Board. 'It seems OK to buy a hardback at £2.50, but dangerous to allow the populace at large to read it at 35p – or that's the way the Board thinks ... I think personally that the Customs Officers want a free read.'

It is certainly a good read. In a small town (un-named, but complete with the weir, the bridge, the

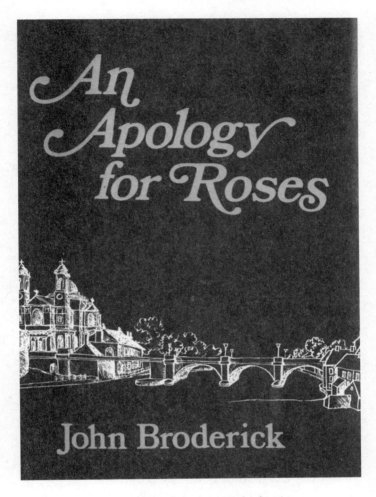

*The jacket of the first edition used a drawing
of Athlone by Anne Murtagh.*

swollen river, King John's Castle) Marie Fogarty is
conducting an affair with Father Moran, the curate,
and another with Brian Langley, one of the travelling
salesmen who supply Fogarty's Wholesale. The affair

with the priest is facilitated by the fact that her parents and the housekeeper go to Mass every Wednesday evening, and further accommodated by covering the statuette of the Blessed Virgin in her bedroom with a handkerchief. But this affair is discovered, and the other inconveniently turns to love. Father Moran is returned to his vocation and his vows by the wisdom of the parish priest, Father Melody, and Marie marries Langley. An unbeatable mixture, then, of sex and religion – but the real engine of the action is money. It is declared as such in the two epigraphs: from Ralph Waldo Emerson the source of the title, 'Money, which represents the prose of life, and which is hardly spoken of in parlours without an apology, is, in its effects and laws, as beautiful as roses'; and Broderick's variation on Thomas Dibdin, 'Oh it's a snug little island! A right little, tight little grocers' republic.' The publishers of the French translation gave it the title, *Le Parfum de l'Argent*. The theme is money as God.

Marie's father, Pat Fogarty, 'accumulated enough money to start his own wholesale business by the time-honoured method of cooking his employer's books.' Agnes Fogarty loathes her husband for the memory of his sexual demands in the past and for the pornographic magazines he keeps in his room – she is effectively killing him by deliberately over-feeding him in spite of his medical condition, on the assumption that she will inherit Fogarty's Wholesale.

Marie works in the office of the business. Only the

proprietor's daughter can be trusted to check dockets and prepare cash for the bank: she enjoys 'the little piles of silver ... the cheques marked on the back with the number of each van-man in case any of them should bounce ... and the crisp piles of notes and dollar-bills from American exiles.' After Pat's death, Marie is truly shocked to find that she, and not her mother, inherits the bulk of her father's estate: 'she was humble about it, like a true believer on whom some unexpected grace had fallen'.

Nelly Fall and Miss Price, another of Broderick's pairs of elderly women who see all and, in this case, are not above moving the action along by sending a couple of anonymous letters, had expected that once Pat died, mother and daughter would 'fight to the death' over the money: 'That's what it always boils down to with them people.' But they are wrong. Agnes Fogarty has to accept the situation, give in to Marie's terms and the fact that her daughter is going to marry a commercial traveller: 'once she had made up her mind to accept the young man she had done so with a good grace. Now that they were all committed to the business and its future a united front was necessary.'

There could never be a fight to the death over the money, because the fight would put the money at risk. Money is to be gathered in, protected, expended only with the expectation of future gain. Agnes makes donations to charity as 'thank-offerings to the god of fortune'. The Fogartys 'entertained little, on the ground of needless extravagance, and casual callers were not encouraged. One never knew who would come to count the house and report their findings to the revenue commissioners.' The affair with the priest has been a threat to the whole structure, but how much of a serious threat could it be, since priests have neither money nor the prospect of money? Normality is restored, money is protected, life can go on; Marie can have a husband, a nice home, and a Crown Derby teaset.

Broderick's narrative skill is as evident as ever, the dialogue as true to the ear as ever with the exception of one excruciating page of overheard lewd conversation between two unnamed men about Marie Fogarty, which is an uncharacteristically clumsy plot-device.

At intervals Broderick inserts wonderful satirical paeans of praise to the god money:

the only God whose existence had not been questioned since the rise of civilisation ... The idol before which the most rampant atheist bowed his head ... the great leveller in whose presence all are equal for no-one knows the day nor the hour that the god may favour the humblest with his favour. Grace from heaven is but imperfectly understood even by the holiest. The blessings that flow from the unseen god of gold are manifest to all.

These insertions are unlike the intrusive authorial comments in other novels, more akin to Dickens' stepping aside from the action to universalize the motivations and persuasions of his characters.

II: A sentient mess

The commercial success of *An Apology for Roses* was unquestionable and the people of Athlone leapt to the task of identifying the heroine. Several young women found themselves pointed out as the original Marie Fogarty, one on the convincing grounds that her family had bought The Willows from the Brodericks in the 1950s.

The critical responses were interesting. Benedict Kiely wrote of Broderick as 'the only Irish novelist who has looked at his people when they are afflicted by the unusual disease of prosperity'. Kevin Casey began his review with a quotation from Georges Bernanos and went on to cite Mauriac, concluding that *An Apology for Roses* was 'a powerful and accomplished novel [with] hints here of even better books to come'. Sean McMahon, on the other hand, saw that 'a fascinating theme was dissipated in a rage against an Irish society which is viewed too personally and pathologically' and regretted that it represented 'no advance on earlier work'. Hugh Leonard wrote of 'overkill' and 'obsessive detestation of provincial mores'.

Broderick himself was interviewed by Eavan Boland just after publication, and reflected on the need to counter both Yeats' 'invented pre-historic Celtic Ireland' and 'the Ireland of the Big House'. He had previously identified the changes in social structures and the emergence of a new moneyed class as the appropriate subjects for contemporary novelists. To Eavan Boland he now said,

There are certain aspects of Irish life – the pretentiousness, the antics of the new rich, hypocrisy – which I definitely dislike. And I think that my first five novels have been more or less negative, they have been attacking things which I dislike about Irish life. But that was something which I had to get out of my system, because I detested these things so much.

That is a revealing assessment by the author of those five novels and clearly indicates an intention to move on – which in fact he was already doing, in a work that had been in hand since at least 1968, but was not to see the light of day for some years to come. In the meantime, he had returned to the literary scene with a bang.

The next few years were to bring major events in Broderick's personal life. The greatest was the sudden death of his mother in July 1974. He had lived with her for virtually all of his fifty years, in an extraordinarily close relationship. On an earlier occasion, when she was admitted to hospital in Dublin following a heart attack, he had stayed at a hotel for several weeks so that he could visit her every day. At her death, he was so distressed that he was unable to attend the interment in the cemetery in Athlone. Living with his stepfather without his mother was soon intolerable – Paddy

II: A sentient mess

Flynn left The Moorings and took up residence in a houseboat on the Shannon; less than a year later, on 3 July 1975, he resigned as a director of the Broderick Bakery Company and his shares were transferred to the name of John Broderick.

In May 1974, and again in July 1975, Julien Green came to Ireland with his son Eric. Green left a fascinating account of the two visits in his published diaries, combining his own responses to Ireland and the Irish with illuminating glimpses of John Broderick as travelling companion and guide. Fr Cathal Stanley was recruited to accompany them as an additional travelling companion and driver. Green refers to the 'jeune prêtre roux, Father Stanley' who rarely got a word in edgeways, but on request would sing Irish songs as they drove, 'd'une voix juste et plaisante'. There was repeated trouble with the car and Broderick managed to run out of water for the radiator in the middle of a downpour. On another occasion, they were sitting on a bench in a hotel garden when a magpie flew past, and as Broderick recited, 'One for sorrow ...' the bench collapsed beneath them.

Green was to write that he could not recall ever having been silent in John's company, and that he had later revisited Ireland in his own way. But their visits were well planned to meet Green's interests. In 1974 they saw Newman House and the cathedrals in Dublin, had lunch with the rector at Maynooth, visited Clonmacnoise, Garbally College, the bookshops of Galway, and Drumcliff, where they disagreed about the merits of Yeats and his epitaph. Broderick would have replaced 'horseman' with 'traveller' in the last line; Eric spoke up for 'horseman' as indicating the speed with which life flashes past.

Julien Green's name was recognized in a Dublin pub and he was greeted with great respect and admiration by 'an emaciated poet ... tubercular, alcoholic', unfortunately unnamed. They also visited Mícheál MacLiammóir, by then half blind, who held Green's hands and recited the Proclamation of 1916, to such effect that even John Broderick was momentarily silenced. In 1975 Green and Eric stayed at The Moorings, and saw Cashel, the Cliffs of Moher and Thor Ballylee, where there was another 'chaude discussion' about W.B. Yeats.

Green records that during their time at The Moorings, Broderick's housekeeper came home from Mass one morning shocked and distressed at having been told that henceforth the Creed would be recited in the form 'We believe' rather than 'I believe'. Broderick and Green shared a distaste for many of the post-Vatican II changes in the Church, particularly where language and music were concerned: Broderick wrote elsewhere about the 'deplorable' standard of music generally in the Irish Church, and the 'acute embarrassment' caused by the poverty of the vernacular language used in the Mass and the 'undisciplined' behaviour of some celebrants. Green had quoted some years earlier a remark by Mrs Broderick, 'Perhaps it is not the Mass we love, but it is still the Mass' – the voice of a loyal Catholic defending the Church in the face of her son's polemic when his aesthetic sense was outraged.

The two polarities of his faith seem to have been Catholic teaching, which he had, he said, taken in through his pores in his childhood home and at his schools, and his dislike of the changes in Church practice that eventually came even to the conservative Irish Catholic Church. In the aftermath of his mother's death he again began to think of entering the priesthood, and got to the point of visiting the English College in Rome, which then, as now, specialized in late vocations. The idea came to nothing, and he turned away enquiries about it by saying that he had been put off by the sight of a large official portrait of Queen Elizabeth II in the room in which he was interviewed.

In a 1974 interview he said, 'I never miss going to Mass, and that includes my years in Paris and London,' but by 1979 he was telling Campbell Spray 'I haven't got faith at the moment ... I do hope the religious experience will come again.' In the same year he caused a stir

in Ireland with an *Irish Times* article that traced the
Jewish, Roman and pagan origins of the Easter festival,
but also criticized the state of liturgy and music in the
Irish Church in terms that reveal his intense irritation
and contempt at 'ham performances at the lectern',
priests 'intoxicated by the presence of a captive audience', and music that 'plays down to the worst instincts
of the people'. A much longer article in 1980 warmly
welcomed the letter of John Paul II to the bishops of the
Universal Church, 'The Holy Eucharist', which was a
blast of the trumpet against excessive ecumenism, a
reassertion of the sacramental nature of eucharistic devotion and the distinction between priestly function and
lay participation, a restating of the doctrine of transub-
stantiation, and a warning of the dangers of 'socializing'
the Mass. Again Broderick returns to the problem of
Church music in particular, saying that 'standards of
singing and playing in Church are, in this country at any
rate, deplorable. This does not mean that they are
unacceptable to God'; they were clearly pain and grief
to Broderick. But however far he strayed from his
childhood beginnings and from the unfailing Church
observance of his mother, he never became a non-
Catholic. In 1984 he told Michael Murphy, 'I am now a
practising, albeit critical, Catholic. Mind you, I always
had an affection for the faith, warts and all.'

On the literary front in the years following *An
Apology for Roses* there were various comings and
goings between Broderick, his agent and publishers

before his next novel reached publication. Calder and Boyars had to be reminded twice in the course of 1974 about payments due to the author – delays caused significant complications because under the Irish tax regime income from literary work was tax-exempt and Broderick's accountants were obliged to keep such income separate, within each year, from his taxable income from the bakery. In any case, Calder and Boyars had already rejected *Oh What a Beautiful City* and nothing had come of an approach to Macmillan. Also in 1974, Pan were negotiating the paperback rights to *The Pilgrimage* and *The Fugitives*, which in due course they published, along with *An Apology for Roses*.

The files of the John Johnson Agency show that by early 1977 the Pan sales figures stood at 24,000 copies of *The Pilgrimage*, 14,000 of *The Fugitives* and 28,000 of *An Apology for Roses*. In 1975 public recognition was added to commercial success in the form of the Annual Award for Literature of the Irish Academy of Letters; in the same year, a new novel, 'Who's that singing outside my door?' was submitted to Macmillan and rejected. It was published as *The Pride of Summer* by Harrap in 1976.

The plot is strong. The central character is Olive O'Reilly, wife of Tony, a midlands building-contractor just breaking into the Dublin big time with all its potential for bribes, kickbacks and general prosperity. Olive leaves her husband and their two children and goes to stay with her elderly cousin Violet Hamilton and her companion Bessie Crane. Tony's brother Frank is called in to act as go-between in the hopes that he will persuade Olive to return home. Olive's presence in their house brings shocking and unforeseen distress to the two old ladies, in part by her husband's design, and she leaves the country, recognizing that she loves Tony but can never again live with him.

Olive, Frank and the two companions are sympathetic and credible characters – Olive strong-minded and clear-seeing about herself and others, Frank innocently attracted by her, Miss Hamilton and Miss Crane drawn with great perception and delicacy – but they are surrounded by a gallery of grotesques and lowlifes. Brother and sister Shaun and Theresa Lucey run a bar in which Theresa collects for the Black Babies while Shaun pimps for rich women in search of sex, and for men (including Tony O'Reilly) in search of heterosexual extremes; he can also arrange abortions. He is not without standards: he instantly ejects from the premises any newcomer exhibiting even a suspicion of homosexual inclination ('We don't want your sort here. This is a respectable establishment'). From the back parlour he and his sister send out vicious anonymous letters and call in 'the boys' of the IRA to deal with any situation that threatens to reveal Shaun's past sexual abuse of their younger sister.

Frank's wife, Kitty, seeking to enhance her sexual experience with her husband, is in contact with a priest in Mullingar who offers her the most detailed and lubricious advice under the guise of marital counselling and signs his letters 'Yours in JC' followed by his initials, V.D. Of Olive's two children, Cathy has an unhealthy dependence on her father and Larry is conducting an affair with the son of one of his father's rich business associates.

A number of minor characters are called by names that parody the names of prominent real-life figures of the day – Charlie McCaughey, Conor O'Brien and others, even a Mary Robinson – without adding anything to the plot or even being amusing in themselves. Much of this reads more as self-indulgence on Broderick's part than anything else, and self-indulgence of a kind that had not previously appeared. It puts *The Pride of Summer* a long way from the control and balance of the first four novels, and it is different also from the entertaining indulgence in exaggerated praise of money that contributed to the effect of *An Apology for Roses*. As such it weakens the Broderick strengths that are also in evidence – the dialogue, the truth of the small-town setting, the set pieces such as the wake-like visits of sympathy by locals to Miss Hamilton and Miss Crane.

And there are other felicities. He paints a charming picture of Frank O'Reilly's two little daughters and their dictionary-game, and in three pages of great technical skill, he delineates first the Church of Ireland rector and his wife, and then Canon Sharkey and his curate, Father Raft, to such effect that in a single appearance they rise off the page and make convincing and illuminating comment on the events around them. Indeed the

Canon and the curate are so realized that they survive
to play major roles in *The Flood* and *The Irish Magdalen* a
dozen years later.

Coming so soon after the success of *An Apology for
Roses*, *The Pride of Summer* was very widely reviewed, and
more than one reviewer addressed the question:
whither John Broderick? The discrepancy between the
sensitivity of the depiction of the two old ladies and the
crudeness of much of the surrounding material provoked
varying assessments. Hugh Leonard, whose review in the
Sunday Independent had the splendid headline, 'Yerra, give
over this Gomorrah on Shannon lark', saw Broderick
'running amok with a shillelagh in one hand and a
hatchet in the other' but conceded in passing that 'the
novel might be accounted an advance on Broderick's
last, and if he could keep his cool ... his work would
improve beyond measure'.

Sean O'Faolain saw the work as having been produced by two John Brodericks – one tough, one gentle.
The tough realist falls into the trap of impersonality
'from which the more subtle Mr Broderick does, thank
God, frequently escape ... the more lyrical or more
imaginative Mr B slaps down the toughie Mr B.'

Douglas Sealy concluded that

if Broderick could get his characters out of their unconvincing
beds and use the space thus freed for a further dissection and
analysis of their thoughts and feelings, not to mention the
whole intricate network of small-town life, his novels mightn't

sell so well, but wouldn't they be better?

Victoria Glendinning, also alluding to the uneven-
ness and shifts of sensibility, wrote:

Mr Broderick's observation is throughout on a higher level
than his writing, which is something of a blunt instrument.
But too many novels are the elegant expression of very little
– his is a fault on the right side.

This only twelve years after Kate O'Brien had hailed
him as 'a master of form' – the drink had a lot to answer
for, if the drink was responsible.

A minor oddity of *The Pride of Summer* is that
Broderick noted at the end of the text the time and
place of its writing, as 'Athlone – Aherlow House
Hotel, Tipperary – rue Vaneau Paris, January–May
1975'. It was the only time he used such notation, which
was more commonly used by French writers, and was
the usual practice of Broderick's great literary hero,
Mauriac. The French connection would have been
much in his mind at the time. He had visited Julien
Green in 1973. *Cité Pleine de Rêves* had been published in
the same year, and rue Vaneau was the address to which
Green had recently moved. There is no indication that
Broderick had made any extended visit in the first half
of 1975, and the mention of the Paris address may have
been no more than a harmless little private conceit,
which would have conveyed nothing to most of his

readers. Aherlow House Hotel in County Tipperary at this time belonged to a partnership that was developing it as a luxury hotel. One of the directors of the partnership was Timothy Kiely, who became a director of the Broderick Bakery Company in January 1974. His fellow directors in the business at that stage were Mrs Broderick, her son and Paddy Flynn. John may well have done some work on *The Pride of Summer* at the hotel – but again there is no certainty, and no real reason for it to be mentioned.

On publication by Harrap in July 1976, *The Pride of Summer* was dedicated to Elena Salvoni, with the words 'who has done more for the arts in London than will ever be known. A small tribute to her wisdom, sympathy and glorious sense of life.' Elena Salvoni is a doyenne of Soho restaurateurs, who at the time was running Bianchi's, later was in charge at L'Escargot and most recently is at what is now called Elena's Etoile, in Charlotte Street. One of the other habitués of her restaurants describes her as 'a sweet, tiny, kindly London-Italian motherly lady', and there cannot have been many of those in the life of John Broderick. He was introduced to Elena by Ken Thomson, who edited *The Pride of Summer* at Harrap.

Like so many of Broderick's friends in the London book world, Ken Thomson remembers him with great affection, recalling convivial evenings full of entertaining conversation, but those who shared such evenings with John Broderick had to be fairly robust. With drink

taken he could become seriously embarrassing and ultimately insensible. Many had the experience of taking
him back to his hotel by taxi and finding later that he
had no recollection of the evening at all; a later editor
decided that he would willingly meet John for lunch but
was not up to evening sessions. Elena Salvoni, though,
still says, 'I loved him dearly drunk or sober,' and others
remember the generous support she gave Broderick at
the time of his mother's death and thereafter.

It is not surprising that he should have taken up
drinking again at that point, and he had been pre-
scribed sedatives in the weeks after his mother's
funeral. Some time after the publication of *The Pride of
Summer* he wrote to Andrew Hewson, who had by then
taken over the John Johnson Agency, that he had just
spent nearly two months in a psychiatric hospital after
again using barbiturates to deal with his insomnia. Most
of his London friends were not aware of this occasionally sombre background to their convivial times.

When Ken Thomson moved from Harrap to Barrie and Jenkins, Broderick moved with him, and Barrie
and Jenkins published his next novel, *London Irish*, in
August 1979. It is set within the eponymous community
– as such it was his first limited step outside his native
Irish setting. The London elements amount to a good
deal of street and Underground geography (which can
be more or less confirmed by reference to an A-Z), to
having two of the characters dine three times in a few
days at (Salvoni's) Bianchi's, and to a smattering of shop

and pub names. The characters, however, are either Irish or outsiders (an American and a Dane, both dangerously exotic).

The central character, Andrew Pollard, is a 72-year-old widower, a property developer who has built up a valuable portfolio based on a small inheritance. His social life is carried on entirely within the Irish Catholic community in London, Irish funerals being the most significant events and the most enjoyed, bringing about reunions with old friends and useful contacts at the customary hotel gatherings that follow the services. Pollard dispenses favours to people from 'back home' in the way of employment or recommendations, and is treated with general respect and deference.

At the outset of the novel, he has just become engaged to Nancy, a blonde American secretary in her twenties. The news brings his niece Rosamund and her cousin Michael over from Dublin as they feel their expectations of inheriting their Uncle Andy's considerable assets are threatened. Equally anxious about the implications of the engagement is Pollard's partner and former employee, Billy Boyd. Boyd is an Orangeman who goes home to Broughshane with his sash and bowler hat every July for the twelfth. He dislikes the idea of the engagement because, at the very least, it will distract Pollard from the business of making and keeping money.

As in *An Apology for Roses*, the engine of the action is money. Pollard's involvement with Nancy is an unprecedented diversion from his usual preoccupations. Normally he assesses everyone according to their attitudes to money and their ability to accumulate it. Rosamund, a successful painter, is seen as doing 'very well with her daubs', but more importantly as having inherited 'a nice legacy' from her father. Michael owns six houses in Dun Laoghaire which, according to his uncle, should have been twenty-four. Michael sets himself to destroy the engagement in order to protect his inheritance; for him 'money gave peace of mind'; money and the prospect of money is necessary for the independence he values above all else, and he is not prepared to compromise his independence by taking a job. He uses the Irish underground network to make enquiries about his uncle's fiancée, and through Mrs Reid confirms Nancy's continuing affair with a louche, bisexual, Danish journalist. Mrs Reid is a suitable Irish widow in her fifties, with sound views on property and funerals and an ability to produce barm brack at the right moment, whom Pollard eventually marries. She further aids and abets Billy Boyd in making sure that Pollard's property is absolutely secure and Michael goes off to the South of France with Nancy and is killed in a car crash four months later. The final scene is the memorial Mass at St Patrick's, Soho Square.

The oddness of the book lies in its tone, or rather in the absence of any characteristic Broderick tone. There is a brief picture of an honourable priest, for once a Scotsman, and a sympathetic picture of Rosamund as

Something in the Head

Photo by P.J. Murray

a creative artist. There is sex in some variety and, as so often, associated with predation rather than love; and there is a suggestion of love recognized and rejected between the two cousins. But there is none of the passion of contempt that inspired the hymns to money in *An Apology for Roses*; none of the luxuriating in lists of possessions and acquisitions; little of faith or its absence; not even any enjoyment or appreciation of hypocrisy – indeed, no enjoyment or fun for the author at all. And of course there is no Athlone, no river or bridge or castle, no streets where everyone knows what is going on behind everyone else's curtains. By the time *London Irish* was published, Broderick had finally severed his connection with Broderick's Bakery, which had been in his family since 1840, and was already planning to leave Athlone – transplanting both his work and himself.

III.

Pray for poor England

*I*n 1986, writing from Bath to his friend Patrick Lawrence, Broderick asked that Lawrence and his Church of Ireland congregation would 'pray for poor England, that it may regain some proper sense of God, the numinous, of first and last things'. But it had not taken him five years to reach his disillusion with England. In 1982, the year after he moved to Bath, he wrote to a family friend,

Of course by now you know that I have never really settled here. I made the bad mistake of confusing London with England. This is the real England, and the natives here are the real English ... they are clever and evasive and sly beyond belief ... dissipated and morally empty, the only thing that means anything at all to them is money. That they worship.

And he was already planning to return to Ireland – 'So

I can't wait to get back to Ireland. Pray that it will be soon.' He never did get back to Ireland to live, and the reasons for the move to Bath are as elusive as so much else about him.

In August 1979 he told Campbell Spray in an interview for the *Irish Press* that he was about to look for a house in the Bristol/Bath area, which would be 'more civilised and nearer London' than Athlone. In the *Sunday Press* in January 1980 another interviewer, Sean Bryson, saw Broderick as 'cut off and isolated' in his large house and as having 'few people to talk to'. Broderick told Bryson, 'I know many people in Bath and there are of course many Irish in Bristol.' For some years after his mother's death in 1974, he would have been liable for tax if he had sold The Moorings and its extensive grounds, but he put it on the market just as soon as he could. In the spring of 1981 he had a heart attack and spent several weeks in hospital in Ballinasloe. He wrote to Andrew Hewson, 'The nurses here are really wonderful, an advertisement for their sex and profession. I really must begin to write about kindness. It is more common than I had supposed.' In October of that year he moved into 10 Russell Street in Bath with his devoted housekeeper, Mary Scanlon. It was, and is, a handsome Georgian terraced house near the Assembly Rooms.

His departure from Ireland prompted a series of press articles and interviews. In one, an interview with Margaret Grennan, he is quoted as saying categorically, 'My reasons for leaving are principally literary,' mainly

10 Russell Street, Bath

that it would be more convenient for him to be nearer his publishers in London, and that he had had to turn down work with the BBC because of the uncertainties of travelling from Ireland – 'every time one thinks of going to see them there is a strike'. Some of his friends thought that he was drawn to Bath by his devotion to

Jane Austen, others that he had previously attended the
Bath music festivals and found a congenial atmosphere;
still others believed that he would have liked to move to
London but found property there a great deal more
expensive than in Bath, and counted on the fast rail
service between Bath and Paddington. In later years
Broderick himself gave other reasons, which are so
vague as to be convincing – that he 'had to leave
because everything was changing', and that 'had he
stayed in Athlone the drink would have killed him'.

Whatever combination of these reasons, and perhaps others, prompted him to leave Ireland, the move to
Bath was not a happy one. Even the rail link betrayed
him. Just a few months after his arrival he fell on a flight
of steps in Bath station and broke a leg. It was apparently badly set, and in spite of several months in plaster
the bones did not knit properly and he was thereafter
unable to drive. The Russell Street house proved to be
too big and inconvenient for Miss Scanlon; it was put on
the market in late 1982 and sold very quickly. Broderick
then rented a house in Dalkey, near Dublin, for several
months, before moving back to Bath in 1983, to a rather
smaller property at 8 The Vineyards. In September 1985
Michael Murphy interviewed him for the *Irish Times*
and reported that this house was on the market:
'Broderick, after much indecision, having finally
decided to quit Bath', and to settle in Dublin or perhaps in Wicklow or Wexford. But first 'he might go to
Mexico for a few years'. This could be indecision, or

8 The Vineyards, Bath

loneliness, or some other unhappiness, or simply Broderick evading an interviewer's questions. In any case, the house was not then sold and he moved nowhere until his final illness took him to a Bath hospital where he died.

The years in Bath were not unproductive so far as

his writing was concerned. Novels were published in 1982, 1984, 1985, 1987 and posthumously in 1991. The first of these, *The Trial of Father Dillingham*, is in several ways the most interesting work he produced at any stage in the thirty years of his writing life.

While *An Apology for Roses* was continuing its commercial and critical success, and shortly before Broderick received the 1975 Award for Literature of the Irish Academy of Letters, *Cité Pleine de Rêves* was published by the Paris publishing house of Plon in a translation by Georges Magnane. Plon had published translations of *The Pilgrimage* and *The Fugitives* in 1961 and 1962 respectively, i.e. in the same years as their publication in English. Plon had been the publisher of Julien Green since his first novel appeared in 1926, and it seems possible that his influence, at a time when he was at the height of his prestige, counted for something in their acceptance of Broderick's unpublished work in 1974. When eventually the novel was published in English with the title *The Trial of Father Dillingham*, it was dedicated to Green, his Christian name given as Julian as he himself always spelled it when he wrote in English.

A number of features of this novel set it apart from, and indeed above, the five previous titles: the context of the action is not family life, the characters are connected by loving relationships, and religious belief is central.

The four main characters are a group of friends living in the four flats of a Georgian house in Fitzwilliam Square, Dublin. They are comprehensively and economically introduced in the first twenty pages. Jim Dillingham arrives back at the house after an extended period spent in Europe researching a book, and the reader is made aware that he is, or has been, a priest. Meanwhile Eddie Doyle, walking home from his office job in Ballsbridge, has dropped in at the Rainbow Inn near Baggot Street Bridge in a sort of painful nostalgia for the days when he frequented such places in search of fleeting sexual encounters 'in the years before he met Maurice'.

Maurice himself, walking home from the shoe shop in Grafton Street that he manages, is recalling the day when he met Eddie in another bar, The Bloomsday, and began the relationship that has lasted for twelve faithful years – but at the same time he realizes that he is going to have to take a taxi in Molesworth Street, physically unable to complete the journey home on foot.

Maria Keeley, the fourth member of the group, formerly an internationally known diva of opera, is the first of Jim Dillingham's friends to arrive at the house, to welcome him in clouds of mink and perfume and costume jewellery and a *mélange* of English, Italian and German, so that as always he was 'as happy as a little boy to see her again'.

Maria Keeley is one of Broderick's great creations. Born Mary Jane Kelly in County Mayo, she was known during her short but brilliant career as Madame Keeley in Ireland, as La Keeley in international operatic circles, and now retired to Dublin, she has become The La. For all her flamboyance, she has the heart and the courage to warn Jim Dillingham of what is to come – that Maurice is terminally ill, but that neither he nor Eddie has been able to tell their friends as yet. So by her mercy Dillingham is prepared for Maurice and Eddie's arrival, and she sweeps them all into a plan to celebrate the reunion by eating together. By this time Maurice has admitted to Jim that he has been 'having treatment', and has confirmed to Eddie that there has been, and will be, no improvement in his condition.

There are several forms of love in the relationships among these four who have come together by a series of chances. Eddie and Maurice, through harsh experiences, have fused love and sex into a bond that is brutally tested, but ultimately not broken, by the manner of Maurice's death. The La loves all three of these men wisely and warmly and practically, understanding their needs better than they do themselves, holding them together when they need each other and commanding their affection and recognition in return (to say nothing of being protected by them and by half the gardaí in Dublin from the consequences of her kleptomania). Jim Dillingham, confused about his priesthood and uncertain about the future, returns to Fitzwilliam Square as to a family. After Maurice's death, it is Eddie's loving perception that prevents him from falling into a sexual relationship with Jim – by contrast, the relationship between Eddie and Abraham Gillespie, whom he first met in the Rainbow Inn, is sexual without any other bond or contact and threatens to tar Eddie with the brush of serious criminal activity.

The differences from Broderick's previous novels, i.e. that the characters are unrelated adults living in central Dublin, as opposed to family members in small provincial towns or suburbs, and that they are bound together by complex, developed and developing relationships, form the context in which the greatest difference becomes apparent: the central importance of individual religious faith.

It had become a cliché to associate Broderick with the so-called 'Catholic novelists' of France because of his known interest in French literature, his admiration for Mauriac in particular and his friendship with Green. His early novels show characters much involved in the practice of religion, conforming to the public and social requirements of attendance at confession and Mass, reciting the rosary and performing the Stations of the Cross, but they are at the same time ever alert to the failure of others to match their own standard of observance. There is occasional evidence of true belief – in Michael Glynn, who is cured at Lourdes; in Willie Ryan, who does not believe but who understands the nature of belief in a much more profound way than his pious family; and in priests like Father Melody in *An Apology for Roses*. Broderick understands the value of the rituals that the Church provides for the extreme moments of life and death, but he has seen also the deadening effect of enforced public performance of rituals unaccompanied by personal faith.

The 'Catholic novelists' (who all disliked the term) were preoccupied rather with the portrayal of individual struggles with faith, individual concern with the state of the soul, consciousness of guilt, failure and unworthiness. Their characters are concerned with whether they are spiritually fit to receive communion, rather than whether their fellow-parishioners will note their presence or absence. Much of their devotion is private rather than public. The Catholic Church in republican, secular France was very different from the Catholic Church of Holy Ireland: its novelists were originally defending the Church against the overt onslaughts of the state and later against the tide of scepticism and scientific advance. But if, as has been suggested, Broderick in writing this work was attempting to reinvent himself as a French-style Catholic novelist, he came close to success.

The word 'trial' in the title has a theological rather than a juridical significance. Jim Dillingham has come to a 'time of trial' in which his quarrel with the Church (over a previous book) has to be revisited, and in which he has to face up to the implications of the sacramental nature of his priesthood, the impulse that makes him renew his phial of chrism oil and his inability to refuse to administer the last rites to the dying Maurice. He is helped by the counsel of his former Bishop, now retired, who by example shows him another way to serve. But the time of trial is not so easily over: he experiences an almost physical revulsion from the very sight of the country church open to receive Maurice's coffin for the funeral, and he has to acknowledge to himself the attraction he feels towards Eddie.

Eddie has to face the tension between his own faith, his love for Maurice, and the implications of Maurice's initial refusal to countenance any priestly intervention as death approaches. He recognizes Maurice's suicide as an attempt to save Eddie from the pain of either having to watch him die without the last rites or having to betray the promise Maurice has exacted from him. Maurice is the non-believer but his rejection of God is almost too emphatic – he is perhaps afraid of the temptation to believe.

The La, at the crisis of the suicide, turns to the faith and practices of her peasant upbringing, still solidly available to her under the fame, fantasy and colour with which her life has overlaid them. She not only knows exactly what must be done for the sake of decency, but knows instinctively that for Eddie's sake it must be correct in every detail. She produces a Third Order habit blessed by Padre Pio and a crucifix blessed by Pope Pius XI (both held in readiness for her own funeral but 'sure I can get another any day'), remembers the necessity for white gloves for the corpse, assists in the laying-out, ensures that the body is not left alone for a minute, makes it clear that they are all going to travel together to the funeral; and so she occupies Eddie's mind in his first grief. Wise in the ways of the world, she knows that Maurice must be buried not in Dublin but in his 'home-place ... with his own people', for the avoidance of any scandal over his life with Eddie.

These are engagements with, for, and against faith on a level that is not approached in Broderick's other books: individual struggles that arise out of credible and consistent characters in convincing situations. What a magnificent piece of work it could have been had the author added one or two more chapters at the end of Part II and thrown away Part III.

The last twenty pages of Part II show all Broderick's technical skill in their rhythm and structure, and it is unobtrusively deployed. The quiet intensity of a brief dialogue between Eddie and Maurice is followed by the sudden violence of the suicide attempt and the frantic efforts of Jim and Eddie to bandage the bleeding wrists; the recital by Jim of the Prayers for the Dying and by Eddie of the Act of Contrition restore a calm in which Eddie recalls the very different deathbed of his mother; the doctor is called and at once understands that he need not complicate matters by mentioning suicide on the death certificate; The La takes over the domestic arrangements; the wake is observed and Maurice's other acquaintances and colleagues come to pay their respects; and they all get themselves to the funeral, each with his own thoughts but united in what they are doing and why.

Then the first page of Part III shockingly introduces

two new characters. Patrick Lord Bellington, 'an Anglo-Irish lordling, claiming to be a Republican, a socialist and an atheist' and his English mistress Kate Vale, a drug-addicted socialite, are in bed on a June afternoon in what was Maurice's flat. The girl in particular is completely alien in her attitudes and indeed her vocabulary to the characters of Parts I and II. They are there as a plot device to bring in the Dublin drugs-related criminal circuit and the Drugs Squad Officer who passes on a warning to Eddie about Gillespie, and who is able to foil a plot to incriminate the tenants of the Fitzwilliam Square house by 'planting' packets of heroin.

In the midst of all this nonsense there is a characteristic Broderick touch when the girl plants the drugs in Eddie's copy of *The Reverberator* and Jim's of *The Sacred Fount*. Not just Henry James, whom Broderick revered, but two of his least-known works. Broderick told Agnes Rook, one of his earlier editors, that if one could get hold of *The Sacred Fount* in one's mind, one could claim to appreciate James.

The heart of Part III is the picture of Eddie without Maurice, and Jim seeking to discern his own future. Eddie's tentative, oblique probing of Jim's feeling for him is surrounded by an extended metaphor of a thief breaking into a locked room, awakening the sleeper within, being recognized, pitied and allowed to escape. None of this needs the new subplot as a catalyst. It is difficult to see quite what went wrong here, why Broderick so completely lost the instinctive sense of form and balance of the earlier novels, and why the English version has a number of variations from the French text.

The variations in Parts I and II are readily explicable. Broderick moves the date of the action from 1956 to 1966 and makes consequent changes in references to prices and to events as occurring in 'pre-conciliar days', not to mention that a character who in 1974 'ressemblait au Cardinal Spellman', by 1982 looked like Cardinal Hume. Some apparent variations arise from errors of translation – ironically 'the R.U.C. in the North' was rendered as 'les catholiques de l'Irlande du Nord'; a 'coffee-table book' was 'bavardage de café'. A number of Irish vernacular expressions escaped the translator altogether: 'I'd be ashamed of my life,' does not necessarily mean 'J'aurais honte de ma vie,' and 'Isn't it well for you?' is not 'Est-ce que ce ne serait pas mieux?' More seriously, 'he was bringing his hatred of the God who made him to the edge of the grave' was translated as 'il emportait avec lui sa haine du Dieu qui l'avait mené au bord de la tombe', which clearly distorts the meaning.

Most significant are the quite substantial deletions from the original text, which occur in Part III. The first group consists of an interrupted reverie by Kate Vale about her dependence on Bellington for the several orgasms per day that she needs and that are the envy of her girlfriends. The next deletions are made from a scene between Eddie Doyle and Abraham Gillespie and show first Eddie's dwelling on Gillespie's superb physical appearance, then his objective assessment of the limits of the relationship, and finally, graphically, his complete sexual submission. And in the last pages the author trims some excess from the metaphor of the thief and the locked room. A case could be made for all these changes, but they are not enough to restore the balance of the novel. The deletion of Bellington and Vale altogether would have been more effective and could have been done easily – as it stands, Part III is considerably shorter than Part I and Part II, and the deletions suggest that Broderick had been dissatisfied with the previous version.

In fact, the records of the John Johnson Agency show that the novel had been around for some time. In 1966 Johnson had written to the author to enquire, 'Any novels in your typewriter?' The response was *The Trial of Father Dillingham* – but in 1968 it was turned down by Weidenfeld & Nicolson, in spite of the success the firm had had with the first four novels, and as *Oh What a Beautiful City* it was rejected by Calder and Boyars in 1973, at about the same time as they published *An Apology for Roses*. (The epigraph to the 1974 edition in French begins with the line 'Oh cité splendide' – the quotation was omitted from the eventual English version and the original title restored. This created some confusion among later commentators.)

An undated typescript in Athlone Public Library entitled 'Oh what a beautiful city', is a longer version, in which Eddie Doyle is the main character. The Eddie of this version is effectively turned into a novelist by the experience of his relationships with Maurice, Abraham Gillespie and Jim Dillingham. Two final chapters show his ending of the sexual association with Gillespie and his distress when, four years later, on holiday in Norway, he learns of the political murder of Father Dillingham in Brazil. By then Eddie has learnt that fiction-writing is a way of absorbing and surviving personal feelings. As he listens to Gillespie, he realizes he can 'look in an impersonal way at something personal in which he was involved', and recognizes that 'a part of his mind was already turning all this to another use'. The news about Dillingham forces him to recall the death of Maurice, but he knows that at some time he will 'use' them both.

There is a lot of Broderick in this version of Doyle. He is described as essentially shy, needing solitude, coming from a family not given to entertaining. Doyle has come to fiction from reviewing, and is credited with having coined the word 'bookjects' to describe the kind of books put together by Patrick Bellington and others; he even has a much-loved little Yorkshire terrier. The Norwegian setting of the deleted final chapter may have been inspired by a visit Broderick made to Oslo and Copenhagen in 1971. All of this has been deleted in ink on the typescript, and none of it survived in the French version. At the very least it is evidence that Broderick repeatedly returned to a novel that was of pivotal importance to him, both personally and professionally.

After the publication by Plon, Broderick seemed to feel less urgency about seeing the work brought out in English, but he came back to it in 1980 and it was again sent to various publishers. Within the space of two or three months it was rejected by Hutchinson, Chatto and Heinemann; in 1981 it was accepted by Marion Boyars Publishing and it appeared in January 1982. Reviews in Ireland ranged from blank incomprehension – complaining that there was no trial in the story, and describing Dillingham as 'renegade' or 'unfrocked' – to recognition, notably by John Kearney and Francis Stuart, of something more ambitious, more literary, more serious than they had seen before in Broderick's work. In the English press, the critic of the *Observer* recognized that Broderick 'gives us the sense of a group of lives long and closely involved', and the *Manchester Evening News* review described it as 'a very compelling novel that cannot fail to make the reader think deeply about the nature and demands of relationships'.

Had this novel been accepted by a publisher in 1968, it would have appeared as the successor to *The Waking of Willie Ryan*, which itself was a clear progression beyond the first three novels. It might have given the author's career an impetus that would have saved him from the 'lost' drinking years that preceded the 1973 publication of *An Apology for Roses*. Instead, by the time it appeared, Broderick had moved to Bath and had already moved on to a different literary path, or paths, with *The Pride of Summer* and *London Irish*.

❧

Throughout these years, he had continued to review frequently for *Hibernia*, the *Irish Times* and the *Irish Independent*. This was solid work, idiosyncratic as ever and owing nothing to any received ideas that might be in the air. He still had it in him to be something of a bruiser in his reviewing as he never could be in his life, and he never gave up or gave in. At the end of 1975 he wrote a review of Heinrich Böll's *The Lost Honour of Katharina Blum* in which he wondered how the author could possibly have been awarded the Nobel Prize for work of so little merit; this provoked several letters of rebuttal printed in *Hibernia*, exposing Broderick's ignorance of the background to the Böll work, calling it 'Mr Broderick's faux-pas review' and 'sour grapes'. The correspondence was enlivened by a letter from County Wexford exhorting Broderick to 'cheer up – you could have been asked to review *The Waking of Willie Ryan*'. He was unpersuaded. When next he wrote about Böll, reviewing a collection of essays, he complained of lack of style, and thought the reprinted Nobel acceptance address typically 'prolix' and 'ponderous'.

This little spat was a minor version of the great Edna O'Brien feud, which gave so much pleasure to readers over a much longer period. It had started in *Hibernia* in January 1971, when a review by Broderick of

O'Brien's *Zee and Co* amounted to a full-page detailed demolition of O'Brien's reputation. He judged that she had 'a notoriety which has nothing to do with litera-ture'; she 'lack[ed] most of the qualities which go to make up a genuine novelist'; her *A Pagan Place* was 'so bad that one wonders how any literate critic could take it seriously'; her talent was 'feeble, utterly unconvincing'; the characters were 'all of them stock characters boiled in a very mouldy pot' and the whole book, 'one of the most embarrassing productions I have ever read'. He had, moreover, written at length about *A Pagan Place* because the work under review, *Zee and Co*, should never have been produced in book form: 'it is a film script ... it contains every known cliché in the English language', and the writer exhibited a 'sloppy view of human rela-tionships' and 'a complete lack of incisiveness'.

Eavan Boland replied to all this, regretting that such an intemperate attack should have come from John Broderick, whom she described as 'a serious [and] a brilliant critic'. He responded in March, moved to reply to 'Eavan Boland ... whom I know so well and admire so much', but retracting little of his criticism of O'Brien.

In 1972 he castigated her *Night* as popularizing and sensationalist, the author as a 'creature of the early '60s' concerned mostly with generating publicity for herself – shades of his suggestion to his agent of stripping naked on the London stage. In 1976 he reviewed *Mother Ireland*, an illustrated volume in which O'Brien sought to create a picture of the Ireland that made her – he admired the photographs, but the author is 'a silly and sloppy writer, the darling of the semi-literates' and the whole work 'a sad book; it is obviously a pot-boiler, and even on that level it is not good'. Most insulting and most telling of all – 'Never was a television career made on so slender a talent.' In 1978 he reviewed the omnibus edition of her work in similar terms, writing of her endless reworking of her single formula, and its appeal to silly readers and indeed silly critics and reviewers, among them Erica Jong (making 'a high ass of herself') and Henry Miller (senile).

In 1979 he suggested unconvincingly to Campbell Spray that the media had exaggerated the animosity between them: 'Of course she has a reputation built on her looks but I don't really hold that against her.' He quoted his mother, who had disapproved of his attacks on O'Brien, telling him that he didn't know what it was to have to make his way in the world. But in case any of this should sound like remorse, he could not resist continuing, 'I saw Edna on a plane recently and I went up to her and said that the bad feeling had gone on long enough. Then I advised her on how to get rid of the age spots on her hands.' That may or may not be true, but it is truly Broderick in interviewee mode. And not everyone would disagree with his assessment of O'Brien's writing.

In October 1980 a radio play by Broderick was broadcast by RTÉ, and the following year was entered for the Berlin 'Prix Futura'. Its title, *The Enemies of Rome*, had first appeared in the Waverley Notebook as a possible title for a novel to be set in a poor and decaying small town, and the very brief outline includes in quotation marks, 'The enemies of Rome are within the Church, not outside it.' Later in the notebook, in an entry subsequently dated as 1965, *The Enemies of Rome* has become a play, the first recognizable version of the eventual radio play.

As broadcast, the action is set in the year 2030, after a coalition of the United States, Europe and China has bombed Russia. The scene is the residence of the proconsul of Italy, who answers to the European Federation in Strasbourg. The Church is being persecuted because of its calls for humanitarian aid for the Russian population, and because the reports of its priests and nuns are the only source of information about conditions in Russia since the bombing. The Pope, elderly and ailing, is in hiding within the proconsul's villa, protected by a number of his cardinals who have infiltrated the proconsul's staff. The concern of the regime is to manipulate events so that the Church will appear to be fomenting violent opposition and so will 'have blood on its hands' and be forced to come to terms with the regime – in return it will be allowed to function to a limited extent and to take medical supplies into Russia. The Pope is shot while attempting to disperse a protesting crowd for their own safety. His successor asserts again that the enemies of Rome can only be within the Church, no external enemy can threaten the continuation of that which is founded on Christ.

The Enemies of Rome was the only play by John Broderick to reach production, although the papers in the Athlone Public Library collection include two other radio plays, a play for television (submitted to RTÉ and rejected), four three-act plays and one one-act play, all in typescript. In 1969 he had mentioned to John Johnson that 'Ray McAnally has asked me for a play', and four or five play 'outlines' appear in the Waverley Notebook.

However, his occasional contacts with the professional theatre were not happy. In 1971/2 the Dublin Theatre Festival was interested in a dramatization of *The Waking of Willie Ryan*, but Richard Condon found Broderick's attitude 'difficult' during the preparatory stages and nothing came of the project. By 1976, when interviewed by Caroline Walsh, Broderick made clear his disenchantment with the Irish theatre in particular, and further declared, 'I want to be the only Irishman who has never written a play.' At that point he had probably written several, but none had been produced. The production of *The Enemies of Rome* and its being entered for a prestigious international competition were something of an achievement, but marked no serious interruption in the flow of novels.

❧

A Prayer for Fair Weather was published early in 1984 by Marion Boyars, just two years after *The Trial of Father Dillingham*. The title is taken from Francis Bacon, referring to the shaking of 'the pillars of government' so that 'men had need to pray for fair weather'. The work is described on the flyleaf as a thriller, but was more often alluded to by the author and others as a spy story. It is first mentioned in Broderick's correspondence with his agent, Andrew Hewson, in 1980, when Broderick was told that although Hutchison had rejected *Father Dillingham*, they 'might be interested in the spy story'. Shortly afterwards, he floated the idea of 'turning the spy story into a satire'. This idea was presumably abandoned; by the time he was interviewed, shortly after publication, by Michael Murphy, the intention was presented as much more high-flown:

I'm by no means the first novelist to comment on the thriller by using the form – Joseph Conrad did so in *The Secret Agent* and Henry James in *The Princess Casamassima*. The spy story is the modern morality play ... The particular point in this book is that those who engage in espionage are all despicable.

In fact, *A Prayer for Fair Weather* is not so much thrilling as completely baffling. Every character is engaged in espionage (including the dog) and the range of possible loyalties for spies is comprehensive – CIA, MI5, FO, KGB, IRA, various Middle Eastern regimes and counter-regimes, Marxist cells of Cambridge graduates. There is double-crossing and double-double-crossing. While not all the characters are entirely despicable, none is engaging and neither is the action.

London Irish was the first novel Broderick set outside Ireland, but its cast of characters was predominantly Irish. *A Prayer for Fair Weather*, with a cosmopolitan cast, occupied London in a different way. It was in part another attempt to get away from the label of 'provincial novelist', or even 'midlands novelist', which increasingly irked him, and to try a new genre as well as a new setting. In the event, there is little sense of the morality of spying, other than that implied by the fact that the strongest motivations are all negative rather than positive, whether anti-semitic, a generalized disgust at 'the state of the country', or a determination to overthrow a 'degenerate society'. This is hardly enough for a modern morality play, and it fails even in the terms of a thriller, since even thriller enthusiasts are hard-pushed to follow the convolutions of the plot without scribbling in the margins. Julien Green, if he ever read it, must have been astounded.

The four novels that appeared between 1976 and 1984 are the only works Broderick dedicated – *The Pride of Summer* to Elena Salvoni; *London Irish* to Adam Lamb, a Church of Ireland clergyman; *The Trial of Father*

Dillingham to Julian Green; and *A Prayer for Fair Weather* to Agnes Rook, who had edited *An Apology for Roses* at what was then Calder and Boyars. Rook, like so many of those who first met John Broderick in a professional context, became a personal friend and had stayed with the Brodericks at The Moorings before Mrs Broderick's death. These dedications represent a fair spread of friendship at a time when he needed his friends.

He never became integrated into any part of Bath society, and indeed never tried to, although Miss Scanlon soon became a devoted and valued member of the local Catholic parish. Broderick travelled to London to socialize with friends from the book world and to attend Covent Garden and other music venues. From the late seventies he had made rather a point of the fact that he 'kept no drink in the house', and this continued during the years in Bath. Interviewers throughout the eighties testify that when he entertained them in restaurants he was most solicitous in seeing that they had all they wanted in the way of alcohol, but drank nothing himself.

When he had occasion to be in London, however, he would stay at a hotel and meet his friends in various establishments, and would sometimes drink very heavily, to the point of having to be taken back, insensible, to his hotel. He could also, as in earlier years in Athlone, cause great embarrassment and anger to some of his companions – he was capable of being loudly and gratuitously rude about people at other tables in a restaurant, or of being exaggeratedly 'camp' in talking to waiters. More than one of his friends can recall occasions when Broderick's behaviour in public became so offensive that they slipped away and left him. He never referred to such events, and may not even have remembered them. In the 1985 interview with Michael Murphy, while again making the point about having 'no drink in the house', he admitted that he did still 'break out' from time to time, 'but very seldom and never for more than a day'. Not strictly true: it seems he sometimes went away for a few days to hotels on the south coast with the intention of drinking. That is another sad John Broderick picture, if true. But unlike the years between 1965 and 1972, this later period did not see the flow of writing dry up.

The Rose Tree was submitted to Marion Boyars Publishers in 1983 and appeared in 1985. The setting is Middle Combe, a pretty village near Bath, with a pub fittingly called The George and Dragon, a bow-windowed antique shop with a suitably homosexual owner, Maxwell Burden, a Dower House and a little stream running alongside the village street. A church with a Norman tower is mentioned, but no priest of any persuasion appears. The exposition in Chapter I is provided by a group of *habitués* in the pub, one of whom later reappears speaking in an exaggerated Somerset accent apparently reserved for the benefit of outsiders. Only two shops are indicated – the antique shop and a sweet shop. But the setting is unimportant. Broderick

The final jacket design, by Christine Emery

was infuriated by the cover design first suggested by the publishers: his title was from Yeats, 'Maybe a breath of politic words / has withered our Rose Tree; / Or maybe but a wind that blows / Across the bitter sea', and he wrote to point out that 'a scene of some cosiness' was quite inappropriate since 'Yeats was not writing about pretty rambling roses.' No more was Broderick writing about a pretty English village.

The story is of Irishman Pat Carron and his daughter May, recently arrived to live in the Dower House and struggling with the effects of an horrific attack some years before in which they saw Pat's wife and older daughter raped and murdered, and were themselves violently abused by three men, IRA supporters pursuing a personal vendetta. The central concern is the psychopathology of May Carron, now twenty-one. Her father's protective care has reduced the damage to the girl and the incidence of her night-time attacks of paralysing fear and shock, but he cannot reverse the 'corruption' of his daughter by the experience, or the distortion of her sexuality. This is recognized by George Duncan, son of Lady Violet, whose own predatory sexuality is such that he is immediately drawn to a potential victim, and May is just as instinctively drawn to him – it is impossible that this should end otherwise than in tragedy.

It is bleak stuff, a far cry from *A Prayer for Fair Weather* and indeed from any other Broderick novel. An outline of the story first appears in the Waverley Notebook with the date 1968, but he did not return to it until he had moved to Bath. It is a short book, the action compressed and the dialogue low-key compared to the emotions swirling below. In contrast to the overheated and overstuffed interiors of the earlier novels set among the moneyed Irish bourgeoisie, the furniture of the Dower House and the contents of Burden's shop are elegant, restrained, chosen with knowledge and discrimination. There are none of the previous Broderick targets of hypocrisy, pretentiousness, or philistinism, but there is an acceptance of the complexities of human behaviour and motivation. The characters are convincing. Pat Carron is aware of the dangers of the exclusive relationship between his daughter and himself, and of the risks to her of moving outside it. Maxwell Burden, who indulges himself in camp clothes and conversation and is ruthless in his buying and selling, is perceptive and sensitive about other people. Lady Violet is attracted to Pat Carron and concerned about May, but loyal to her son.

There are occasional oddities and lapses in the writing, discrepancies in description of characters, clumsily ungrammatical sentences that testify to Broderick's known unwillingness to revisit any of his work at the behest of his unfortunate editors and perhaps also to his deteriorating health and increasing unhappiness. In 1982, just after the move to Bath, he had had to write to Marion Boyars that he could not go to the United States on a trip arranged to promote sales of *The Trial of Father Dillingham* because of trouble about the capital gains tax on the sale of The Moorings – whatever the difficulty was, it was not finally settled and continued to give him trouble.

Just as *The Rose Tree* was being published, Broderick wrote a lengthy article for the *Irish Times* about the city of Bath, its old ladies (either witches or ageing dutiful daughters or discarded mistresses) and their attendant gigolos and their snobberies ('they are never at ease with the Irish'); about the tourists who invade the town for ten months of the year; the falseness of the Georgian facades; the awful climate and the dust. Even Broderick finally recognizes the logical conclusion of all this spleen – 'the reader might well ask ... "If he hates it so much, why does not the bleeding fella get the hell out of it?" ... but that is another story'. Five months later he was talking to Michael Murphy about his decision to leave Bath.

Although he never left Bath, he did in another sense return to Athlone. He returned to the very first pages of the Waverley Notebook and the first mention of the story that was to become *The Flood*. Since 1970 he had been talking of 'a large novel' about his home town and its people. In 1973 he told Eavan Boland that it would 'have to be set in the Athlone of thirty years ago, but it will be written with love'. As the subject recurred at intervals in the notebook, it was expanded to form a trilogy, and at one point it seems as though the third volume might have been set thirty years later than the first two. In 1980 another Broderick article for the *Irish Times* under the title 'Redeeming the time' contrasted the Athlone of his childhood with the town as it was at the time of writing, just as he was preparing to leave it.

The inevitable changes, such as the growth of the town in size and population and the increase in motor traffic, were less important to him than the changes in his own micro-geography. The old wooden shop fronts had been replaced with vitrolite and glass, few of the old shop names remained in Connaught Street, Cox's orchard had disappeared, St Peter's Church in Chapel Street had become the Dean Crowe Hall and been replaced by the large new church in the square (where young John Broderick served at the first Mass in 1937) and there were no longer 'ass carts in Connaught Street and herds [*sic*] of sheep on the Batteries'. The context of his childhood no longer existed for the children of 1980s Athlone, but he could recreate it, and in doing so reach back beyond the context in which he found himself in Bath, and beyond the contemporary contexts of his earlier novels. *The Flood* was quite specifically set in 1933. It was ready for the publishers in 1985.

The recreation of Athlone was extraordinarily detailed. The name of the town was changed to Bridgeford, and much of the action was set in the Duke of Clarence Hotel, in reality the Prince of Wales Hotel. But any reader could walk around the streets of Athlone today following the directions given in *The Flood* and *The Irish Magdalen*. Connaught Street, Chapel Street, Main Street, Pipe Lane, Church Street and Mardyke Street are all unchanged; the bridge, the castle, the Friary and the Father Mathew Hall are all in place. Broderick's pen turned the Dean Crowe Hall back into

St Peter's, with a loving description of the galleried interior and the in memoriam plaques in the porch. The Father Mathew Hall was turned back into a cinema, rather than the Public Library, and Cox's orchard was restored, as were the gaslights. The extremes of poverty known in the thirties were also recreated, the fear of the County Home such that it could hardly even be named, the relentless grind of living without any possible provision for emergency and the burden that it laid particularly on women.

But the recreation went a good deal further than that. When *The Flood* appeared, Athlone readers above a certain age recognized many of the characters as being drawn very directly from life – this gave rise to some amusement and considerable outrage. Many who read the book, and no doubt many who only heard about it, never forgave Broderick, and it was at least part of the reason that several who had known him since his childhood refused to attend his funeral in Athlone just two years later. One such person says that the funeral was 'boycotted by Connaught Street, including some of his own family'. *The Flood* was the last straw, after the drinking, the 'eejiting-about' and the departure to England.

A third recreated element, after the topography and the characters, is more problematic. Broderick reproduced the vernacular of Athlone in a mixture of phonetic transcriptions and malapropisms. It is deployed with all his linguistic skill, its use allowing for precise gradations among characters, some of whom easily use standard English when it is in their interests to do so or when it suits them to differentiate themselves from their companions, but it is not easy for the non-native to read on the page, occasionally comes close to incomprehensibility, and can be simply irritating, especially the constant 'dis, dat, dese, dose'. One reviewer called it an 'improbable patois', but it remains problematic because there are those in Athlone who swear it is an exact reproduction of their own playground, as opposed to classroom, language.

The plot is one of the basic plots of fiction – the outsider coming into a community with an agenda of his own and failing to realize that the community too has an agenda, to which all its members more or less subscribe. Added to that are some of the Broderick basics – the linked lives and shared history of a small town, the known rituals, the jungle-drum communications, and the particular Athlone basic of the river Shannon. The incomer, an Englishman named Slyne, seeks to buy a stretch of land along the river, which is owned in small parcels by a variety of locals: three elderly women from the poorest part of the town, the owner of the Duke of Clarence Hotel, the resident 'boots' at the Hotel acting on behalf of his wife, the owner of O'Farrell's Bar and Grocery, and a local returned from America who has made his fortune at Tammany Hall and is assumed to have been the confidant of teamsters and presidents alike. The significant role played by the Shannon is that it floods the relevant area of land for three months every winter, but Slyne views the land in June and plans to build on it. Benedict O'Farrell, the publican, savours the event in retrospect,

You never saw so solemn an Englishman in your life. And the bunch of twisters he was proposing to do business with, right in the middle of the bog on the finest day of June that ever was, all of us double-crossing one another like eels in a box.

Slyne is a lamb to the slaughter. '"We won't fall out over a perch or two, will we?"' he says to the sellers.

They all laughed. They would cause someone to fall off a cliff, or hold his head under the river water, over less than a perch, but of course the Englishman had to be humoured.

O'Farrell and his wife Ellen are wonderfully sympathetic characters, a loving couple whose bar and grocery is also a drop-in centre, citizens' advice bureau, benefits office and social-work department before any of those institutions were ever heard of. As Broderick wrote in the 1980 article, in those days 'we did not have to attend seminars about community spirit: it was there, as naturally as the air we breathed'. The three elderly women are fierce rivals and inseparable old associates. The notion of the money to come awakens their fantasies. Mrs Susannah Braiden, known to all as Hosannah, works out the details, ' "I'm goin' ta do a roun' of de churches, startin' wid de pro-Cathedral an' endin' wid

Adam and Eve's, an' I'm goin' to light six large candles in each place for de sins o' de world, and for me salvation."' Mrs Prendergast, known as Mrs Pig, being the widow of a pig-dealer, asks if Hosannah will stop at Dublin.

'A course not ... I'm goin' to Mullingar, Tullamore, Roscommon, Ballinasloe an' mebbe Galway to do de same. I'm goin' ta surround dis pagan town wid holy lights, burnin' at de foot of God for all de sins I see committed, permitted and provoted in dis dangerous town o' Bridgeford.'

'"Promoted, I suppose you mean,"' says Miss McLurry, who has pretensions (and no nickname) and is going to spend her windfall on Paris modes.

There are reversions to the style of some of the first Broderick novels. He describes Mrs Daly's private sitting-room at the hotel, all velvet curtains, Persian carpets, mahogany, lacquer, Spode, Sèvres, in which she worships the illuminated scroll of the family tree of the Dalys

from Murrough Mor O'Dalaigh and his bride, the Princess Emer of Dalchaise, both of whom flourished two centuries before Christ, according to this manuscript hand-painted by nuns ... Mrs Daly's name had been Slattery ... But she had completely identified herself with the Dalys. Her preoccupation with them was that of an enthusiastic convert to a new religion.

A political meeting in the Square follows a ritual course to the point where an apparently murderous fight breaks out between the supporters of the two sides. The Guards

with perfect impartiality marched off six men to the barracks in Excise Street behind the Castle; three from the Cosgrove supporters, three from the opposing camp. There they would be given strong tea, and a teaspoonful of poteen to help sober them up. No charges would be brought. They were put to bed on blankets in the one cell the station boasted of, and unless a wife came along in a towering temper and demanded her man, they would be left to sleep peacefully until the morning.

And in this, the last novel he completed, the craftsman Broderick tries out a new device; the occasional insertion of a paragraph of stream of consciousness in italics filling in the lightning impressions and reactions going on behind the words of a speaker.

There is little doubt that it was 'written with love', and with hope also, but *The Flood* was refused by Marion Boyars Publishing in 1985. It then went on a dispiriting round of other publishers, being refused by Secker and Warburg, Collins Harvill, St Martin's Press, André Deutsch, Century Hutchinson, Hamish Hamilton, Bodley Head and Viking, before finally returning to Marion Boyars and being accepted.

In the months preceding its appearance Broderick had more than once mentioned other possibilities to Andrew Hewson. In January 1987, in a letter which was principally about the need to look for a new publisher, he wrote, 'I have two short novels of Bath finished,' and in March he suggested 'a collection of short stories'. A typescript in the Athlone Public Library collection seems to be one of the 'short novels of Bath'. The cover page is handwritten, ' "The Man from Meroe" by John Broderick 17th April 1986 – 14th June 1986', below which, also handwritten, is 'W.R. Adamson' and the date '2/2/87'. A second cover page is typewritten 'The Man from Meroe by W.R. Adamson' with the hand-written addition, 'a.k.a. John Broderick'.

The plot is developed from one of the brief out-lines in the Waverley Notebook. In a group of five out-lines headed 'Bath stories', number two reads 'Woman who brings a black to live in her flat in Russell Street' and the possible titles include 'The Man from Meroe'. The 'black' in question is the eponymous man from Meroe, an Oxford-educated lawyer who moves into a flat in Bath with a young Englishwoman, also a lawyer. Among the other tenants are two specimens of the old ladies described in Broderick's 1985 article. What with their dislike of living under the same roof as a 'nigger', 'black' or 'darky', and the useful Freemason contacts of another tenant with the letting-agent and the employer of the man from Meroe, the young couple are quickly 'persuaded' to leave Bath. Bath is not flattered in the picture Broderick paints, and there is little evidence that he took any great pleasure in the writing. The pos-sibility that had it gone to the publishers it would have done so under a pseudonym suggests a degree of distancing by the author in the months when he was awaiting the appearance of *The Flood*, which was so close to him. But writing was his trade and he still felt the compulsion to practice it – at least until he saw the reaction to *The Flood*.

It appeared in September 1987. By the end of October Broderick was writing to his agent to say that he was depressed by its reception, and not planning to write again. Reviewers in the Irish press were savage: they hated the use of the local vernacular, were unamused by the comic effects, thought the theme overworked, found it at best sentimental and at worst crass. Broderick was accused of racism, whether for portraying 'an intelligent Englishman and a collection of thick Paddies' or because he showed 'a devious Englishman defeated by the superior wiles of the townsfolk'. He was further accused of snobbery and contempt for his characters. Worst of all it was described as 'a tale presumably written for the English market' – that must have been the hardest for him to bear, and the farthest from the truth. It was really written for himself, and was scarcely fiction at all, indeed it might have been written as memoir and sounded a truer note. (He even put himself into the book – he said later that the long, hilarious description of a young man in the grip of a stupefying hangover was drawn from experience.)

As memoir it might also have received more attention in the English press. Broderick wrote to his publishers expressing his disappointment at the lack of reviews in England, and was assured that review copies had been sent out. He found some consolation in a 'rave' review by D.J. Taylor in the *Independent*. When Broderick read Taylor's own first novel the following year, he wrote to congratulate and encourage him, and they met just a month or two before Broderick's final illness, Broderick still generous with his time for young writers.

The second volume of the planned Bridgeford trilogy was already well in hand before *The Flood* appeared. As *Canon Sharkey and Father Raft* it had recurred several times in the Waverley Notebook, with notes of characters and scenes developed over the years. In the event Broderick was unable to get it to the point of publication before he died, but Marion Boyars, with the help of Andrew Hewson, completed the necessary correction and editing and it appeared in 1991 as *The Irish Magdalen*.

The story is complete in itself, but figures from *The Flood* reappear, and the picture of Athlone is as accurate as before. Canon Sharkey of St Peter's and his curate Father Raft are the principal characters, the Canon being instantly recognizable to Athlone readers as Dean Crowe, who raised most of the money to build the present church in the square. Canon Sharkey's fund-raising method is a sweepstake, run from a disused classroom in the convent school by a 'kitchen cabinet' of faithful women of the parish. Tickets are sold throughout the country and, through names and addresses supplied to the Canon by good Catholic girls working for the Bell Telephone Company, all over the eastern seaboard of the United States. Any interference by the Mafia in the American arm of the business is quickly put down by the Canon's network of good Catholic mothers of Mafia bosses. Father Raft greatly disapproves of most of his superior's activities, is bitterly aware of his own inferior position, and is ever alert to any slight or absence of due respect. The title *The Irish Magdalen* derives from the fact that when the Canon's housekeeper dies he replaces her with a young woman who has been trained to cook by Mrs O'Flaherty Flynn at the Duke of Clarence Hotel: the girl, unfortunately, is the half-sister of a famous local prostitute known to all as Polly Pox, and the story is fed to the American press where it appears under the headline 'An Irish Magdalen' and is designed to discredit the Canon and his sweepstake.

There is a lot of Broderick at his best here. The action rattles along, propelled by endless criss-crossings of the town by Donie Donnelly, Diddler Dunning, nuns, devout parishioners, Father Raft and others. An American is locked up drunk in a bedroom in the hotel and given poteen (under the guise of local mineral water) to help his hangover. Four men are sent by their wives to remonstrate with Canon Sharkey about the unsuitable housekeeper, and find at the end of the confrontation that they have accepted his gracious offer to bless the new swimming pool that Father Raft is promoting, and altogether failed to mention the housekeeper. A splendid procession makes its way to the site of the proposed pool through streets bedecked with flags and banners and grottoes and makeshift altars, all most critically commented upon by the devout members of sodalities and Children of Mary who form the procession. The stream of consciousness inserts have disappeared, and the vernacular language is somewhat restricted, indeed a loving couple temporarily fall out when the girl infers that her young man is criticizing her speech:

'I alays tout dat ye were stuck ub because ye tink ... dat ye spake like d'English ... I can pronounce me dis, dat, dese, an dose juss as good as you can ... Only people dat wands ta run down de Irish makes out dat we spake like dat. An' doan try to make liddle a me.'

The reviews would have given Broderick little consolation, with the possible exception of the article by Declan Lynch in the *Irish Press*. Lynch admitted to being an Athlone native, and vouched for the accuracy of the Athlone patois. He paid tribute to the book's 'wonderfully comic virtues'. Broderick's comic gift was often unacknowledged over the years. Perhaps the Irish are too accustomed to their own fluency and felicity of speech to recognize the skill with which he transferred it to the page, and perhaps English reviewers, underexposed to that everyday fluency, thought Broderick's version invented or exaggerated. The vernacular of the last two novels was something of an aberration, but the dialogue of the earlier novels gives an extraordinary vitality and variety to his characters. Lynch also recognized that 'Broderick is clearly having great fun in this delightfully penetrating novel' – the author would have appreciated that perception. And with luck he might have laughed to see himself summed up as 'Athlone's finest writer' – how strong was the competition? Who could rival his thirty years of journalism, reviewing and novel-writing, his experimentation with themes and techniques, his resisting of the temptation to repeat the commercial success of *An Apology for Roses*, his devotion to the craft?

❧

Broderick's last year brought him lingering illness of a cruel kind. In June 1988 he was interviewed at his home in Bath by David Hanly for the RTÉ television series *Hanly's People*. Broderick looked rather older than his years, overweight and unfit, and sat uncomfortably in a large armchair, his hands constantly fidgeting.

Many of his answers to Hanly's questions confirmed what was already known – that he had long intended to return to Ireland, that he had been shocked and disappointed to discover the dishonesty and general low morality of the English, that he had had a sheltered childhood surrounded by women until being sent away to school, that his great resources had always been books and music, and that he had started writing while still at school. Hanly asked a series of questions about Broderick's sexuality, which he answered very briefly but clearly: he was not homosexual but bisexual, he had never been sexually promiscuous, and it had not made life difficult because he 'had not been ruled by the sexual impulse'. It was clear from his demeanour that he found the questioning intrusive.

Asked about religion, he said that his childhood experience of the Church had given him lifelong moral principles and a sense of right and wrong, and though he had 'for years' been uncertain of his belief, he had (by 1988) returned to regular attendance at Mass and confession and tried to persist in 'doing his best every day'. He confirmed that he had never drunk alcohol until, at the age of thirty-two, he was introduced to gin at a Dublin social occasion. He had never 'got into any major trouble' through drinking, since in Ireland such things could always be covered up (and on occasion 'the Guards would take you home'), but the struggle against alcoholism had been very hard, particularly the indignity of admitting to it, and the impossibility of drinking 'socially'.

Looking at the recorded interview now, the viewer is struck by several things. Broderick's idea of his return to Ireland would almost certainly have been disappointed – he saw himself in Dublin or Wicklow, returning to live among the amusing, quick-witted, honest

Irish people with their awareness of Christian values: this is as romantic as the idea of moving to Jane Austen's Bath had been in 1981.

His account of how he spent his days – reading for reviewing purposes in the morning, doing his own writing after lunch, watching the television news at 6 pm and later hearing the Irish news on the radio – shows a solitary man still working at his craft, even after the bitter disappointment of the reception of *The Flood* the previous year. Asked whether he was 'a happy man', he politely disdained the question, saying that no life was entirely happy or unhappy and that it was misguided to search for happiness.

Finally, the interview itself is disappointing. Hanly's approach, while not aggressive, is trivial and unsympathetic, with no appreciation of his subject's immersion in literature and music and no space to develop any one of half-a-dozen ideas thrown out by Broderick, which could have filled the time available with great interest. When it became known just two months later that Broderick had had his first stroke, a number of his friends were quite sure that it had been precipitated by the strain of doing, and then watching, the interview.

In August he had a fall on the staircase of his home in The Vineyards and was taken to hospital – it is not clear whether he had a stroke, which caused him to fall, or vice versa. He made a partial recovery from this first attack, but was left with some paralysis of one side. He was, according to an old friend who visited him in hospital in these weeks, an uncooperative patient, complaining about his treatment and refusing to persist with the necessary physiotherapy. He even failed to make proper arrangements for Miss Scanlon to look after the ordinary household expenses, until another friend intervened. It was thought that he might be discharged to a nursing home to convalesce and eventually recover sufficiently to return to Ireland. He was able to spend a few days in his own house at Christmas 1988, but he was sad and lonely and clung to any visitors, wanting them to stay longer and to promise to come back.

Before any arrangements had been made for him to return to Ireland, he had a second stroke. This time there was further paralysis, his speech was badly affected, and he was mentally confused. Those who visited him in the hospital at this stage, among them Marion Boyars and Ken Thomson, found that it was difficult for him to make himself understood, were not always sure he understood them, and saw that he was clearly distressed. He died on 28 May 1989.

Photo by Michael Geraghty

Epilogue

*J*ulien Green was not the only commentator to speculate about what Broderick might have become. Patrick Murray, in a long article published in 1992 in the journal *Eire-Ireland* wrote, 'I have sometimes felt that he should have devoted his talents to the literature of travel and to the higher journalism rather than to fiction. Broderick might have become a major practitioner of these forms – an Irish James Morris perhaps.' Other reviewers expressed a quite personal disappointment at some of his unsuccessful work and felt, like Green, that Broderick had never quite known what he was doing. He said more than once that he 'didn't give a hoot' about anyone's opinion of his writing but, having reviewed hundreds of novels by others, he was not incapable of judging his own and he was right to see *The Waking of Willie Ryan* as his best and most complete single work. He did not claim that it was a masterpiece, or that he was an unacknowledged genius – his vanities were personal and not professional. Professionally, as well as personally, he was both engaging and elusive, endearing and maddening: finally, astray in Bath, he cocooned himself in the Athlone of his childhood and saw himself reviled for it.

The obituaries that appeared in the press were every bit as contradictory as Broderick himself, starting with the fact that his date of birth was almost universally given as 1927 rather than 1924. He may have introduced this error himself – it first appeared on a book-jacket in 1965 – and he certainly never corrected it, whether out of a wish to knock three years off his age or just out of his preference for imprecision about his personal life. The *Daily Telegraph* obituarist wrote that Broderick was 'born in 1927', 'notoriously irascible', and 'wrote a novel in French', all of which were untrue. The obituary ended with the ineffable final paragraph: 'He was unmarried.'

The *Irish Times*, although its obituary contained a number of factual errors, published in addition an appreciation of Broderick by Brian Fallon, who as Chief Critic had been responsible for commissioning much of the author's reviewing for the paper, and recalled a man who was 'kind and generous, though he liked to veil this side of him at times with a catty and sharp-tongued humour', and who 'might have made as good a critic of music, particularly opera, as he was of literature'.

Ronan Farren saw the novelist as 'a sad figure who

never really found his *métier*', but concluded 'his criticism and book reviews were always erudite and witty, his company enjoyable'. The *Westmeath Independent* called him 'somewhat of an enigma to many in his home town', but acknowledged 'his immense pride in his Athlone heritage'.

That pride was very evident in the terms of Broderick's will, drawn up and signed in Bath on 29 November 1988. After generous provision for Miss Scanlon for her lifetime, he bequeathed all his books, records, discs, tapes and a portrait drawing of himself by Sean O'Sullivan to the Westmeath County Library Service, to be placed in the Athlone Branch; a sum of £40,000 to create a fund to provide assistance to students from Athlone studying at University College Galway; and eventually the residue of his estate to the Arts Council of Ireland on trust to use the income for 'the benefit and assistance and advancement of the Arts in Athlone'. There was also a single small legacy to the parish priest of St Peter's for masses. Broderick would surely have enjoyed the ensuing correspondence. The solicitors wrote to St Peter's to enquire as to who should receive the cheque for masses for the repose of 'Mr Broderick's sole'. Canon Murray wrote back presuming that Mr Broderick's concern would have been for his soul, and the solicitors had the grace to reply confirming that, to their knowledge, 'the late Mr Broderick did not own a flat fish nor have particular concern for the under-surface of his feet'.

Other than that given to his housekeeper, there were no personal legacies at all. It was not the first time he had shown his appreciation of the library service. When he was leaving Athlone in 1981 he donated books, photographs and a portrait by local artist Peter McCabe, and when the contents of The Moorings were auctioned he heard that the library had bought another painting, *Eel Weir at Athlone* by Paul Henry, and returned the cheque, effectively donating the work. The library also has custody of Broderick's unpublished typescripts and manuscripts and a large collection of press cuttings of his published reviews, other occasional journalism and interviews.

In May 1999, ten years after his death, Athlone reciprocated with the first John Broderick Weekend, organized by the Rotary Club through a group chaired by George Eaton and having as its secretary, appropriately, the librarian Gearoid O'Brien. The opening Mass was celebrated in St Peter's on Friday 28 May. On Saturday morning there was a ceremony in which a street was named 'John Broderick Street' – the triumphant result of negotiations with the local authority. At the Prince of Wales ('Duke of Clarence') Hotel four papers on Broderick were presented by Desmond Egan ('Broderick and Athlone'), Patrick Murray ('The Irish novels'), Brian Fallon ('Remembering Broderick') and D.J. Taylor ('The last years').

On Saturday evening, dinner at a fine restaurant on the shore of Lough Ree was followed by a discussion of

From left to right: *Simon Cavanagh, President of the Rotary Club of Athlone; George Eaton, Chairman of the John Broderick Committee; John Walsh, Town Clerk of Athlone; Most Rev. Dr John Kirby, Bishop of Clonfert; Mrs Mary O'Rourke, TD; and Councillor Mark Cooney*

'Broderick the cosmopolitan' and on Sunday there were guided walks around parts of the town significant in the life and works of Broderick, including The Willows and The Moorings. It was a splendid tribute from those who had known and admired him, and there was much speculation about what he would have thought of it all.

In the absence of any sign of disapproval from beyond the grave the Committee published the seminar papers and organized a second Weekend in 2001. On this occasion the opening service in St Mary's Church of Ireland church was addressed by Broderick's friend the Rev. Patrick Lawrence, then Archdeacon of Meath. There followed a civic reception at the castle and a seminar in Athlone Little Theatre, including papers by Madeline Kingston, Dr Eamon Maher and Patrick Murray, who at the behest of the Committee considered money, sex and religion (respectively) in the novels. The dinner on this occasion was attended not only by participants in the seminar and other interested individuals, but also by representatives of the companies whom the Committee had succeeded in persuading to sponsor the venture. The intention was that the John Broderick Committee should continue its work in one form or another, perhaps by developing the John Broderick Weekends into a wider Athlone Literary Festival while retaining a Broderick element. The publication of this biography and the timely reprinting of *The Pilgrimage* and *The Waking of Willie Ryan* by The Lilliput Press are evidence of the Committee's success in pursuing its first objective, which was to make the best of Broderick's work accessible again.

But it should not be thought that only Athlone remembers John Broderick. In January 1991 *The Pilgrimage* was republished in Paris as *Le Pèlerinage* by

Editions de la Découverte with a lengthy preface by Julien Green in which he recalls his long friendship with the author.

In 1994 Marion Boyars Publishing had a query about the film rights to *The Pilgrimage* from the Paris agent of the actress Charlotte Rampling. Rampling then collected a copy of the English version of the novel from the publishers in London. Had the film ever been made, the sight of Charlotte Rampling as Julia Glynn would have gone a long way to erase from the memory the dreadful cover picture used on the Pan paperback edition. Throughout the years since his death various articles have been devoted to Broderick in a variety of publications, notably by Patrick Murray and Eamon Maher. In June 2000 a paper entitled 'John Broderick – an Athlone author in search of a European home' was accepted at a conference of the International Association for the study of Irish Literatures and was received with particular interest by American and Australian participants.

Broderick made no claim to be a great writer, nor is the claim made on his behalf by those who do not wish to see him forgotten, but the sheer variety of the memories that remain of him – as generous friend, knowledgeable critic, music lover, amateur actor, alcoholic, traveller, raconteur, social irritant, literary craftsman and indeed eejit – paint a picture of a complex Irishman who could justifiably claim to be a writer, who produced some fine and some bad novels and a great deal of good reviewing that led readers to great works by other authors. The craft of writing is what holds his story together, as it held him together throughout an often unhappy and unsatisfied life. Could he have seen his own life whole, as no one ever can, the writing would have been what mattered to him, what weighed heaviest in the balance.

His personal pride would have been wounded by the fact that only about a dozen people were present at the cemetery in June when he was buried. Many in Athlone had their reasons for not attending, and the Irish can sometimes be ambivalent about those who choose to leave Ireland, whether or not they find success by so doing. But he would have welcomed the one-word description of himself – 'Author' – which is engraved on the family headstone.

Bibliography

Quotations from Broderick's novels are taken from the following editions:

The Pilgrimage (Pan 1975).
The Fugitives (Obolensky 1962).
Don Juaneen (Panther 1965).
The Waking of Willie Ryan (Panther 1969).
An Apology for Roses (Calder and Boyars 1973).
The Pride of Summer (Harrap 1976).
London Irish (Barrie and Jenkins 1979).
The Trial of Father Dillingham (Marion Boyars 1982).
A Prayer for Fair Weather (Marion Boyars 1984).
The Rose Tree (Marion Boyars 1985).
The Flood (Marion Boyars 1987).
The Irish Magdalen (Marion Boyars 1991).

I have also quoted from two articles by Broderick published in *The Fountain*, the magazine of Garbally College: 'The stained glass window' (1967) and 'The novel' (1969).

Quotations from the journals of Julien Green

published in Paris by Plon are given in my translations.

Banned in Ireland: Censorship and the Irish Writer, a collection of interviews edited by Julia Carson, was published by University of Georgia Press (USA) in 1990.

I have drawn extensively, particularly for the first part of this book, on a series of articles by Gearoid O'Brien published in the *Westmeath Independent* in June/July 2001.

Of the large number of reviews, articles and interviews relating to Broderick's life and work published in various newspapers and magazines, I have quoted in particular from those detailed below. Details of all other articles and reviews mentioned, as well as unpublished work by Broderick, are listed in the bibliography compiled by Gearoid O'Brien with the support of Westmeath County Librarian Ms Mary Farrell, and published by the Library Service in May 1999, under the title *John Broderick, 1924–1989; Towards a Bibliography of His Writings*.

ARTICLES BY JOHN BRODERICK

'A curate's egg at Easter', *Irish Times*, 14 April 1979.
'Letter from Rome', *Irish Times*, 19 April 1980.
'Bath bricks', *Irish Times*, 18 May 1985.

DISCUSSION

'The future of the Irish novel' (J.B. with Terence de

Vere White, Kevin Casey and Richard Power),
Irish Times, 8 January 1970.

INTERVIEWS

J.B. interviewed by:
Caroline Walsh, *Irish Times*, 29 May 1976.
Michael Murphy, *Sunday Independent*, 26 February 1984
and *Irish Times*, 3 September 1985.
Campbell Spray, *Irish Press*, 16 August 1979.
Sean Bryson, *Sunday Press*, 27 January 1980.
Margaret Grennan, *Sunday Press*, 30 August 1981.

Index

Index